KV-013-478

EDUCATION TODAY

History Teaching Through Museums

A list of titles in the EDUCATION TODAY series
will be found on the back cover of this book

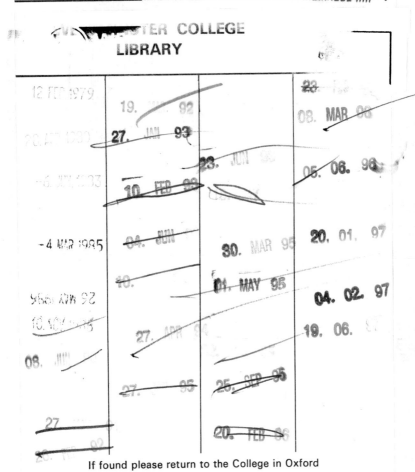

History Teaching
Through Museums

JOHN A. FAIRLEY

LONGMAN

LONGMAN GROUP LIMITED
London
Associated companies, branches and representatives throughout the world

First published 1977
ISBN 0 582 36307 1

Printed in Great Britain by
Whitstable Litho Ltd, Whistable, Kent

FOR MARJORIE

Contents

Preface

The task of writing this book has been particularly pleasurable, for it has provided numerous opportunities to return again to favourite places, as well as to visit others for the first time. Above all else, however, one thing which has emerged is the extent to which, in recent years, there has been a revitalizing of so many of the institutions with responsibility for the preservation of the tangible reminders of our historical heritage. Nor is it simply a matter of modernised display techniques, for the freshness of approach which has so characterised recent initiatives in museum work has encompassed whole new attitudes of mind. There was a time, not so very long ago, when the museum visitor was expected to keep his distance and, in numerous ways, was often denied the chance to derive the maximum benefit from a close examination of the exhibits. If anything is to be taken as typical of the changes, it must surely be the increasing recognition of the need to maximize opportunities for the intellectual enrichment of the visitor, young or old.

In the generosity of the welcome, some museums have gone further than others along this road. Understandably, some find themselves often in situations where the need for caution is greater than it might be elsewhere. One does not, for example, allow groups of schoolchildren in unlimited numbers to rampage unrestrainedly over anything and everything in sight; there must be established limits, within which access is permitted but beyond which it is not. It is in the determination of those limits, however, that the imaginative curator seeks to reconcile the necessity of safeguarding his precious exhibits with the principle of extending to all the fullest opportunities to examine and enjoy them.

Recently, I had the rare privilege of being present at the opening of a new museum. It was in Washington D.C., where, on 1 July 1976, President Gerald Ford formally inaugurated the National Air and Space Museum as a superbly fitting memorial to America's bi-centennial year. No superlatives could properly do justice to this wonderland of technological glories, but they were there for all to see—the Wright *Flyer*, Lindbergh's *Spirit of St Louis*, John Glen's *Mercury* capsule, the *Friendship* 7 craft, the Apollo 11 command module *Columbia* and many more. Unobtrusively set to the right side of the entrance hall and standing on its own was a small exhibit stand, displaying only a triangular-shaped fragment of dark grey stone. The stand was not railed off, nor was there any protective cover over the exhibit. Out of everything there, it was this un-assuming item which most intrigued my eight-year-old son, for it was accompanied by a caption plate which read, quite simply, 'A specimen of rock brought back from the moon'. But that was not all. The stand carried an additional caption, in some ways as remark-able as the main one. More than anything else in the vast new complex, it was this which somehow seemed to symbolize the final bridging of the gap between attitudes of prohibitive conservation and those more properly concerned with the extension and enlarging of human experience. It was a simple message of just two short words, 'Please touch'. Needless to say, a very thrilled eight-year-old boy was only too happy to oblige.

John A. Fairley

Acknowledgements

The preparation of this book has been undertaken at a time when local authority areas have been undergoing a major restructuring. As a consequence, a number of schools museum services have been given new names and, where possible, these have been incorporated in the list which follows. The manuscript, as originally submitted to the publisher, was as up-to-date as it could be at the time, but it is possible that in the interval between submission and publication, some additional changes in nomenclature may have taken place.

Acknowledgement is made to the following schools museum services for help willingly given: British Museum; Commonwealth Institute; Victoria and Albert Museum; Bethnal Green Museum; Geological Museum; National Army Museum; National Maritime Museum; Imperial War Museum; Museum of London; Geffrye Museum; Passmore Edwards Museum, Newham; Horniman Museum and Library; Brighton Museum; Southampton Art Gallery and Museums; Reading Museum and Art Gallery; Portsmouth City Museums; Wiltshire County Library and Museum; Carisbrooke Castle and Museum; Buckinghamshire County Museum; Luton Museum and Art Gallery; Oxford City and County Museum; St Albans Museums; North Hertfordshire; Hereford and Worcester County Museum, City Museum Bristol; Devon Schools Museum Service; Ipswich Museums Educational Services; Colchester and Essex Museum; City of Norwich Museums; Birmingham City Museum and Art Gallery; Gedling House, Notts; Leicestershire Museums, Art Galleries and Record Service; Derby Museums and Art Gallery; Derbyshire Museum Service; Manchester Museum; Merseyside County Museums; Warrington Museum; North Western Museum of Science and Industry, Manchester; Grosvenor Museum, Chester; Yorkshire

Consortium, Wakefield; Bradford Industrial Museum; Leeds City Museum; City of Sheffield Museums department; Hull Museums; Bowes Museum, Barnard Castle; National Museum of Wales; Haverfordwest County Museum; Glasgow Museums and Art Galleries; Dundee Museums and Art Galleries.

Help received from the staff of the following is also acknowledged: Science Museum, South Kensington; The *Cutty Sark*; HMS *Belfast*; The National Gallery; Dover Museum; Anne of Cleves House, Lewes; The Tramway Museum, Crich; York Castle Museum; National Railway Museum, York; Lewis Textile Museum, Blackburn; Rochdale Co-operative Museum; North of England Open-Air Museum; Welsh Folk Museum, St Fagans; Ironbridge Gorge Museum Trust; David Livingstone Memorial Centre, Blantyre; Museum of Childhood, Edinburgh; Nationalmuseet, Copenhagen; Roskilde Ship Museum; Museu Artes Populares, Lisbon; Smithsonian Institution, Washington; Denver State Museum, Colorado; Queen Mary Museum, Los Angeles; Department of the Environment; National Trust; National Trust for Scotland; Royal Mint.

Special thanks are also due to the following, whose assistance was invaluable: Victoria Airey, Christina M. Harris, Mary Speaight, Eric J. Woodward.

We are grateful to the following for permission to reproduce illustrative material: City Museums and Art Gallery, Birmingham, page 125; G. F. Gold, Jordanhill College of Education, pages 151, 152, 153 and 154; Trustees of the British Museum, pages 142 and 143; Museum of Costume, Bath, page 75; County Museum, Council of Hereford and Worcester, pages 147, 148 and 149; Foundry Trade Journal, page 135; Ironbridge Gorge Museum Trust, page 40; The John Judkyn Memorial, Bath, page 118; Leeds City Museum, Leeds, page 110; Museum of London, pages 5 and 6, 132, 134, 137, 138; London Transport, London, page 51; Mount Vernon Ladies Association of the Union, Virginia, U.S.A., page 61; National Army Museum, London, page 73 *left and right*; Sussex Archaeological Trust, pages 144 and 145.

1

The Educational Purpose of Visiting the Museum or Historical Site

Generations of those who in their youth were addicted to the escapist literature of the juvenile comic may well recall how the adventures of their youthful heroes and heroines were often played out against recurrent backgrounds and repetitive situations. In recollection, one such plot springs to mind, in which the circus is coming to town and the local children are looking forward with great delight to the wonders of the 'Big Top'. Alas, their hopes, no sooner formed, are destined to be dashed because although the circus in all its glamour and spectacle will be functioning on Saturday afternoon, their schoolteacher has other plans for them. This authoritarian figure, of stern visage (the female of the species invariably wore pince-nez!) has alternative ideas about how they should spend Saturday afternoon and these centre upon visiting of all places—a museum. Ugh! Understandably, the plot as it unfolds in the colourful comic strip is concerned with the childrens' collective and, ultimately, successful efforts to outwit the teacher; the final frame invariably showed a deliriously triumphant group occupying the best ringside seats, wearing fancy carnival hats, and tucking in to large, beribboned boxes of chocolates, as the trapeze artists up above or the clowns down below went through their paces. The unfortunate implications behind all this were, of course, that in contrast with the circus, which was clearly and with justification understood by all to be a place of joy and delight, the museum was dull, boring, unattractive and certainly not to be reckoned as a place in which children might seek to spend any part of their leisure time.

Fortunately, this image has changed, partly in consequence of more outward-looking methods of teaching, particularly in the primary school, but mainly in consequence of the growth of schools museum services as well as a revolutionary improvement and increased sophistication in techniques of museum display.

Such changes are perhaps more apparent in museums than historical sites, although both types of place have been affected for the better. The distinction between the museum and the site will be dealt with more fully in the following chapter. Here it is enough to say that in many respects they stand for different ways of presenting the same thing. Both represent tangible reminders of a past that has gone forever. In one sense, and in common with primary documentary material, they enshrine the only real elements of historical survival. By contrast, historiographical works that are today regarded as standard sources of reference can become insignificant tomorrow, either in consequence of the weight of further disproving evidence, or even simply because the views and opinions expressed have in the meantime become academically unfashionable. This is not to denigrate in any way the significance and value of historical scholarship, but simply to stress the point that what does not change are the stones of Old Sarum, the mosaic pavements of Fishbourne, the Elgin Marbles in the British Museum or the Nelson collection of the National Maritime Museum at Greenwich. True, our appreciation, even our regard for such things may alter and be tempered according to outside factors, not least the importance which we ourselves or, indeed, contemporary society may choose to attach to certain persons, events and happenings in the past. Nevertheless, the humblest piece of Norman masonry, the most insignificant worm-eaten Tudor beam or the simplest and commonest of eighteenth-century taper holders has a charisma that stems from an awareness that it is a tangible link with the past.

Historical writing is an attempt to produce an imaginative reconstruction of the past. The good historian can, by this process, take us back in time to a former age and, by his own peculiar blend of skill, direct a spotlight on what he considers to have been the major events, the watersheds, the turning points in the human story. The analogy of the spotlight is only too real, for there is so much that must remain in darkness, so much that cannot be illuminated, however hard the historian may try. But to hold in one's hand the red-sealed officer's commission, issued on the last day of 1759 by George II to Samuel Moore, Gentleman, appointing him to be Ensign in Captain Sandford's Regiment of Foot, signed at top left in the King's own hand, bearing the countersignature at bottom right of his leading minister, William Pitt, and folded in such haste as to produce on the surface a partial mirror-image of the King's signature, is to experience a fresh sensory dimension of historical awareness. With this simple act of handling and observation goes the knowledge that famous men, for long well and truly established 'in the history books' once passed that same piece of vellum from hand to hand, each in turn reading and then signing the document. There is a similar compelling magic about being able to handle a piece of a Roman amphora and to pick out on its inside surface the four parallel grooves left by the potter's fingers, or to trace the intricate design carved on an eighth-century Assyrian cylinder seal, and to note the integrated artistry of its clay impression.

All such experiences provide the one thing which the historical textbook, however imaginatively produced, cannot—a real and tangible emotive link with the past. This is the fundamental inspirational value of visiting a museum or historical site: the sense of immediacy, and of contact with, for example, the stirring days of the Armada, which can come in the perspective of a well-preserved sixteenth-century Spanish helmet, or the imagined echoes of battle which can be inspired in the mind at the sight of bleak, inhospitable Culloden Moor.

To consider the visit to museum or site in this way is to seek forms of expression which will have relevance for the development of the student's imaginative awareness—what some educational philosophers have called the affective area of development. Cognitive growth, on the other hand, may be equally well fostered by the presentation of opportunities to identify, classify, sketch, measure, compare, contrast and handle exhibits. No amount of careful textbook explanation of the working of a Boulton and Watt engine can provide an effective substitute for seeing the real thing in action in the Science Museum at South Kensington. Of course, ideally one would hope that both types of source, textual as well as museum, would contribute towards effective cognition, the one supplementing and extending, rather than being regarded as an alternative to the other. In the same way, although textual material is undoubtedly invaluable, comprehension of the relative size of the Stonehenge complex can take on a new significance when experience is extended by an on-the-spot look at the site itself.

Now, to say all this is to make claims for a certain kind of experience which is enjoyed and appreciated by many people other than schoolchildren. Our great museums and sites of historical interest are patronized regularly by all sections of the community. One has, for example, only to visit the Castle Museum at York on any Sunday afternoon, in order to see this. Nevertheless, our present concern is to try to determine the particular place which a visit of the kind envisaged might have within the context of schoolwork. Perhaps the simplest way of answering this is to say that where possible it should be integrated into a larger study. Thus if any kind of historical investigation is being undertaken in class—whether it be called a project, patch, study topic, etc., is of no particular consequence—it is reasonable to assume that research activity will be diversified. Implicit in such diversification is the idea that much that is valuable as stimulating, useful and, above all, firsthand source material will be found outside the classroom, and the museum or site are logical places for this.

The isolated and unrelated visit has little to commend it. The fact that it could trigger off a hitherto unrecognized interest, or perhaps plant the seeds of a particular, albeit slow-flowering intellectual growth, destined at some later indeterminate time to bear fruit, need not be in dispute. At best, however, this is a consequence likely to affect only a small minority, while at worst such a visit can turn out to be little other than a working-hours diversion which, in one sense, would put it in the same category as fire drill or a visit to the dentist.

Where, on the other hand, the visit is placed within the natural context of an enquiry which may lead the student to a variety of possible sources, its function should generally prove to be of much greater value. There are two reasons for this. In the first place, the concrete evidence available for examination at museum or site can readily be related to appropriate references in literary material such as parish records, census returns, letters and diaries, or to pictorial recording that might range, according to the chronology, from tapestry and stained glass to painting and photography. The complementary advantages of this marriage of sources can be most valuable, for the tangible evidence of museum or site can so readily invest the printed word with a fresh reality, while, on the other hand, much that is strange or puzzling in the archaeological remains can often be clarified by reference to the written source. In illustration of this point, and notwithstanding the fact that work directives will be dealt with more fully in a later chapter, the following item of work material from the former London Museum shows how effectively this can be planned.

Samuel Pepys and the Fire of London

Sept. 2nd 1666

    Jane called us up about 3 in the morning to tell us of a great fire they saw in the City . . . so down with a heart full of trouble to the Lieutenant of the Tower who tells me that it began . . . in the . . . baker's house in Pudding Lane and that it hath burned down St Magnus' Church and most part of Fish Street already.

Look at the model in Room 9. Why should the flames be spreading so rapidly?

    The King commanded me to go to my Lord Mayor . . . and command him to spare no houses but to pull down before the fire every way.

How would this help to put out the fire? In Room 12 find and draw a tool for pulling down houses. Study the other fire-fighting equipment on display. Which would be most effective?

Sept. 2nd

    River full of lighters and boats taking in goods . . . and only I observed that hardly one lighter or boat in three that had the goods of a house in, but there was a pair of virginals in it.

Draw something from Rooms 10 or 11 which you think worth saving.

Sept. 5th
> I up to the top of Barking Steeple and there saw the saddest sight of desolation that I ever saw; everywhere great fires, oil-cellars and brimstone and other things burning.

Study the painting of the Fire in Room 11. Pepys's view from Barking Steeple must have been something like this. Imagine you are standing beside him. Describe what you see.

After the Fire
On 8 September Pepys wrote
> People speaking their thoughts variously about the beginning of the fire and the rebuilding of the City.

In Room 12 find plans for rebuilding London. Name three men who put forward ideas. From photographs and prints find out what changes were made to streets and houses when London was rebuilt.

Fire insurance
In Room 12 find out the name of the man who introduced Fire Insurance into England.
In Room 16 find firemarks of the Insurance Companies; draw and name two below.

The interest here, relative to the point being made, is that the documentary extracts are from eye-witness accounts contained in the diary of Samuel Pepys. The museum contributions are diverse—a large working diorama, seventeenth-century fire-fighting equipment, paintings, prints, domestic furnishings and so on. This unpretentious directive has been put together with considerable skill, and clearly the compiler was consciously aware of the very considerable advantages to be derived from drawing on as wide and interacting a range of sources as possible. The implications for resource based learning will be obvious. The tapping of interrelated source reference points in this way is something which should always be positively encouraged and which is all the likelier to develop in situations where there is a good relationship between the schools on the one hand and the museum services on the other. Many times it will emerge naturally from the course of study itself. On other occasions it may be more contrived. For example, Merseyside County Museums Education Service offers, among other things, intramural study sessions on the theme of the nineteenth century, designed to back up and support work done at school in what is known to be a popular period of study. Museum-based activity includes the viewing of slides, handling small specimens and work in the galleries. From a number of sub-themes with such titles as costume, children, travel by sea, etc., teachers may choose the particular aspects most appropriate in the light of what has been undertaken in school. This interaction can subsequently continue as more of the museum material is introduced to support further school-based study.

So much for the first of the two advantages claimed for a visit that is not isolated in itself, but related to a wider and broader based academic scheme. There is, however, another merit in this, and it is that by placing the visit firmly within a recognizable context of study, the teacher may avoid giving the impression that there is some particular mystique about such an activity. It is true that it requires its own special form of organization and that the skills which trained enquirers are expected to employ within the context of museum or site are not wholly identical with those which are regarded as appropriate to the classroom. Nevertheless, in historical terms, the ultimate objectives of any historical enquiry conducted both in and out of school should be consistent. Understandably, of course, teachers may disagree as to the nature of teaching goals and the degree of emphasis to be placed on particular aspects. Most, however, would probably accept as a working hypothesis that such goals would be concerned, in part, with developing in pupils the skills needed to undertake the task of understanding something of the past and, in part also, with developing a feeling for and an interest beyond the statistics, in man's life and work at a particular stage or stages in the human story. These are, in other words, aims which encompass both the cognitive and the affective. Within that framework, all relevant sources have an equal validity and the museum or site visit is thereby brought into proper perspective, taking its place alongside the literary or pictorial record as one of a number of reference points that can both inform and inspire. The pupil who is attuned to this notion is likely to move all the more easily and readily from one source area to another—whether it be library, county archive office, textbook, picture gallery or museum—without feeling any fundamental difference in the nature of one search location as against the next, but rather seeing all investigatory

possibilities as holding together in the most natural of inter-
dependent relationships.

This last point is germane to the question of when exactly the
museum visit should take place. No single answer can be given, for it
depends almost entirely on the nature of the historical enquiry. In
some instances, it may be appropriate to trigger off interest in a particular area of historical study by an initiatory visit. In others, it
might be better to introduce it at some natural point in the middle
of the project, when pupils have already acquired a basic understanding of the theme and acquaintance with sources, and have also
become sufficiently motivated to be likely to gain the maximum
benefit from a visit. In other instances, it might be more appropriate
(sometimes as much for practical as for educational reasons) to keep
the visit until the end. In other words, if the intention is to inspire
and arouse interest, then an early acquaintance with the museum is
desirable. If, on the other hand, the interest is already tapped and
assured, then there is nothing better than the visit which comes
fairly late on in the project, when pupils are well informed and ready
to respond to much that is already familiar to them from alternative
sources. Perhaps one of the most justifiable examples of this latter
procedure is in relation to the Mediterranean school cruise which has
become a popular type of educational excursion within the last
decade. The author well remembers while on a family holiday to
Athens being astonished at the sight of busload after busload of
British schoolchildren arriving from a cruise ship anchored in Piraeus
harbour. From snatches of conversation overheard it was obvious
that many had been well prepared for their trip, so that the thrill of
the first walk up the steep steps through the Propylaea to the culmi-
nating splendour of Parthenon and Erechtheum was enhanced, not
only by the feeling of surprise which always accompanies that first
sight of one of the world's wonders, but also by a confirmation of
what the mind was already attuned to receive and to respond to.
There can be no doubt that the pleasure to be derived from such an
experience will invariably be immeasurably enhanced if it is based on
a foundation of acquaintanceship, however vicarious, and however
derived.

To speak of the visit as initial or final is to oversimplify a host of
possible arrangements. There is no virtue in stereotyped patterns of

work. In many circumstances an initial as well as a final visit has much to commend it. Yet again, the progress of the study may take such a form that the pupils pay a succession of visits in order to extend or consolidate work previously undertaken, or to supplement enquiry which is being conducted in other directions. Furthermore, where special exhibitions are mounted for a limited time, the school may have to modify its plans and accept the opportunity to visit when the material is on show, even though the time may not be ideal.

Whatever the arrangement decided on, it should be impressed on the pupils that the visit is in the nature of a privilege, and neither an imposition nor an irrelevant diversion. To have the opportunity to be in such immediate contact with firsthand material, or to be taken to the place where it all happened, is an experience to be treasured, particularly as it is the closest that we may approach to sensing what has now become part of our heritage. Good historians may be able to present a fully comprehensible account of the Battle of Trafalgar, but there are few better ways of capturing the atmosphere than by walking the gundeck of HMS *Victory* herself.

One final point: the last thing which the museum visit should become is a kind of annual treat. Something which is seen as entertaining and recreative but only peripherally related to the mainstream of the child's education. On the contrary, the attitude to be encouraged is that the museum may be one of a number of agencies which can provide some of the resources needed to instruct the child as well as to stimulate him and enrich his learning.

2
Types of Museums and Historical Sites

This is probably an appropriate point at which to consider the various possibilities for outside visits. The matter will be treated by dealing first with museums and then with historical sites.

Museums

In considering their potential usefulness, it is important to appreciate that museums can differ considerably in function and character, and this often determines their value in a particular context. In any attempt to establish general categories there is the danger of over-simplification, but broadly speaking it is possible to distinguish three principal forms of museum organization which we may call 'comprehensive', 'folk' and 'specialist'.

Comprehensive collections

Museums in the first category are numerous, but they vary considerably in size. On the one hand, there is the small general collection, such as is represented by the Dover Museum with its eclectic range of exhibits, including lepidoptera, ceramics, pottery, natural history, local history, horology, medals and other bygones. At the other end of the scale, some of our most famous museums, particularly in the bigger provincial towns, offer wide coverage, with whole areas within them given over to specific types of collection, so that exhibits range from archaeology, ethnology and local history to natural history, science and industry. One example is the Bristol City Museum, which has collections of Egyptology, British archaeology, ethnography, natural history and geology. Another good example is that of the Royal Scottish Museum in Edinburgh which has the most wide-ranging display under one roof of all British museums.

Archaeology, geology, art and natural history are all represented. The Natural History Department has much historical material from early explorers and modern habitat groups; there is also a Childrens' Gallery. Technology, too, is well represented, with an excellent selection of accurate scale models that can be operated by the visitor. There are large shipping and mining halls, and galleries dealing with navigation, aeronautics, space flight and general science; there is even a Radiation Corridor.

How valuable is the comprehensive museum to the teacher? It is difficult to generalize with certainty on this, but the small ones are probably likely to be the least useful to teachers whose classes are pursuing particular projects. This is because the chances of finding relevant material in sufficient quantity to make a significant contribution to the study are not high. The converse is that the larger comprehensive collections are generally more fruitful, but even in the big city museums particular areas can often prove to be disappointingly meagre, yielding at most only a small case of relevant material. From the point of view of a school wishing to undertake the study of a particular topic in depth, the comprehensive museum with its relatively thin spread of material obviously poses certain problems. It is true that within some of our major institutions of this kind it is often possible to find a specialist collection of respectable size, but this cannot be guaranteed throughout the museum. On the other hand, provided the museum is a sizeable one—and in many cases even where it is not—the major advantage of having access to a place of this kind is that the teacher will usually be able to find something that is relevant to the period being studied. This is the strength of the comprehensive collection: the fact that it is generally possible to find some points of contact, however few, with widely differing study topics. Bearing this in mind, probably the most effective way of using a comprehensive museum is to relate the investigation to exhibits which illuminate the appropriate historical background. If, for example, a class was undertaking a study on the voyages of Captain Cook it is unlikely that the nearest comprehensive museum would be able to furnish directly relevant material. On the other hand, there is every possibility that children could find out about aspects of late-eighteenth-century costume, kitchen utensils, silverware, pottery, firearms, agricultural implements, ships, navigation, or whatever else the museum had to offer. This would enable them to round out their picture of England in Cook's time and thus effectively supplement their specialist studies. The fact that a museum with a comprehensive collection cannot contribute specifically to the pupil's knowledge does not mean that it should not be used. On the contrary, a background awareness of the period concerned can enrich and illuminate aspects of a project that might otherwise be overlooked. It is for this reason that teachers are recommended to explore the possibilities of using such places even in support of highly specific studies.

Specialist museums

In terms of our provisional classification, the second broad category is the specialist museum, wherein emphasis is laid on a particular range or class of exhibit. Such museums have become increasingly common and they are probably the ones of most direct value to the teacher pursuing a school project which can be linked to the specialism concerned.

Some are national institutions. For example, the aim of the Imperial War Museum is to record and illustrate all aspects of war, including British and Commonwealth countries, from 1914 onwards. Its departments include weapons, uniforms, vehicles, field guns, aircraft, models and dioramas, with reference departments housing large collections of photographs, paintings, posters, film, books, documents and maps. Among the exhibits are countless items of interest to children, such as 'Ole Bill', one of the 'B' type London buses used as troop carriers on the Western Front in the First World War. Boy Jack Cornwell's Victoria Cross, Lawrence of Arabia's rifle, V1 ('Doodlebug') and V2 missiles from the Second World War and a Spitfire which saw action in the Battle of Britain are also there. Periodically the Museum mounts special displays which have great popular appeal, for example the Colditz exhibition of spring 1974 and a Home Guard exhibition in the following autumn.

The National Railway Museum at York is another example of a specialist museum which is world-famous. It is concerned to display railway relics of all kinds. Locomotives, dating from 1829 take pride of place, and the original collection is to be extended in the light of the recently completed reorganization and rehousing of the Museum.

Historic carriages include everything from the earliest open type of the 1840s to the ultimate in mobile luxury that characterized the royal saloons of Victoria, Edward VII and Alexandra. Supporting exhibits—signalling apparatus, uniforms, posters, tickets, etc.—make this a perfect mine of information for children engaged in associated study topics.

These are examples of two large and important museums specializing in particular subjects. Many other museums in the specialist category are not nearly so extensive, but they are just as interesting and, in the correct context, equally appropriate. Thus, the Jewry Wall Museum in Leicester has an excellent range of archaeological exhibits from prehistoric times to 1500, with mosaics *in situ*, the Geffrye Museum in Shoreditch is a permanent exhibition of furnished period rooms, extending from 1600 to the present day, and the Museum of Childhood in Edinburgh, through its collection of toys, dolls, games, books, costume, medicines, comic books, hobby kits and other paraphernalia deals in a warmly nostalgic way with childhoods that are gone.

Some specialist museums, such as the Florence Nightingale Museum at Winslow or the David Livingstone Museum at Blantyre, choose to focus attention on famous personalities. The latter is an example of a centre run by a private trust, and the whole complex, with its World Fountain, its reconstructed weaver's cottage, its African huts, wood carvings, notes and manuscripts, and the well-thumbed pocket Bible carried by Livingstone on his last journey, is a memorial to the man whose vision and faith did so much to advance the frontiers of human knowledge.

One obvious advantage in making use of the facilities of any specialist museum is the probability that there will be a more than adequate amount of material exhibited. Museums of this kind often have good reserve collections, linked to loan services, and this is another reason why they can be valuable support agencies for school-based history projects. Not only can the display collection be exploited within the museum, with all that this implies in respect of caption information, printed guides and the use of worksheets, but the work can also be effectively extended, through loan resources. These are not only intrinsically valuable in the sense of making a positive contribution to the study, but also help to provide a physical link between classroom and museum. Loan services are dealt with at greater length in Chapter 6.

Of course, there are specialist museums where there is no question of using reserve collections, since the whole function of the place is to provide the opportunity for participation and 'experience'. One of the best examples of this is the Tramway Museum at Crich, which is sited in the open and is very much a working museum. This remarkable venture began in 1959, with the acquisition by the Tramway Museum Society of a derelict limestone quarry in Derbyshire. It was here that a three-quarter mile track was laid, and, during the season when the museum is open to the public, something like one-half of the present unique collection of over forty tramcars make regular runs with visitors aboard. Trams which formerly ran on the systems of the major provincial cities of Britain are well represented—Sheffield, Hull, Leicester, Leeds and Glasgow—and there are also a few from Oporto, Vienna, Prague and Johannesburg. Plans for a full-size Edwardian street at the main terminus are well under way, and the fine Georgian façade of the Old Derby Assembly Rooms now stands facing a stone-paved area with an iron tram shelter, Victorian gas lamps, an Edwardian bandstand and the gates which formerly belonged to Marylebone Station in London. The whole effect is most pleasing and lacks nothing in historical authenticity.

Folk museums

The third broad classification is that of the folk museum. Here the concern is usually to illustrate various aspects from the past and present life of the community within whose locality it is situated. Arts and crafts are invariably well represented, and this can encompass many activities, from style of buildings, furniture, tools and implements to music, painting, drama and any other appropriate type of cultural activity. Some of the best examples of this kind of museum incorporate two features: first, the reconstruction or re-erection of actual buildings, and the furnishing of them in an appropriate way; secondly, the provision of opportunity to witness the demonstration of old crafts. In the development of this imaginative type of museum the Scandinavian countries have played a leading part, and the preservation and revival of all that is best in the cultural and domestic life of their communities has had a significant influence upon the taste and design of modern Scandinavian products. That the most sophisticated furniture and glassware in modern Europe is of Scandinavian origin is due in no small measure to the influence of the many folk museums which have done so much to bring about the marriage of modern technology and the traditions and craftsmanship of the past. For the school pupil, the breathing of life into the community's past is fostered even more in many such places by the encouragement given to children to try out for themselves the ancient craft processes. At Lejre in Denmark, for example, classes are regularly taken to the local open-air folk museum where, at various points in the grounds, facilities are available to operate a small blacksmith's forge, to fire pottery in a primitive earth kiln, to make bricks, or to prepare vegetable dye in a large pot.

Our own folk museums have not yet reached this level of active school participation, although some comparable and interesting experiments have been undertaken in this direction. Nevertheless, the nature of our school curricula is now such that it is generally probable that most children will at some point in the syllabus undertake the study of the locality, either for its own sake or as a starting point for some other theme. The educational value of a folk-based collection is therefore, considerable. Museums in this category are to be found throughout the country, and there are three particularly fine examples in Britain, which are worth a short mention, as illustrative of the way in which this kind of well-planned museum can make an effective contribution towards school-based work that is particularly concerned with local study.

The Welsh Folk Museum

One of the most outstanding examples is the Welsh Folk Museum at St Fagans, which is a part of the National Museum of Wales. Here, for example, one of a number of re-erected exhibits is the eighteenth-century Esgair Moel woollen factory, within which all the machines date from the late eighteenth to the mid-nineteenth century. The fact that this machinery is worked by water power provides an opportunity to rediscover at first hand all the processes—carding, spinning, weaving, fulling and dyeing—which were characteristic of the methods employed in those far-off days when the mill was originally sited at Llanwrtyd in Brecknockshire. The practice also of producing by those processes bed quilts, rugs and cloth woven to traditional Welsh patterns is an additional bonus for schools undertaking studies concerned with the folk life of the past. There are, in addition to the woollen factory, a number of re-erected farmhouses and cottages, together with a tannery, tollgate house and smithy. As representative of traditional Welsh crafts, woodcarving and coopering are carried on and the products are sold to the public. In the galleries the exhibits illustrate the domestic, social and artistic life of Wales, with an extensive collection of kitchen utensils as well as the material relics of dairying and laundering. Interesting objects associated with Welsh festivals and saints' days are also represented and, not surprisingly, material relating to the folk institution of the Eisteddfod. For the Welsh schoolchild, St Fagans is a rich quarry and here he will find much in which to take pride.

The Beamish Open Air Museum

The Beamish North of England Open Air Museum in County Durham is in many respects similar in concept to St Fagans, in that the purpose is to illustrate something of the past life of its community in an imaginative way. In this case the focus is on the industrial, agricultural and social history of the north of England in the late nineteenth and early twentieth centuries, so that it has a smaller chronological coverage than the Welsh museum. Part of the interest of this museum is that it is at a fairly early stage in its growth and a five-year development plan is envisaged, so that by 1979 it is hoped to have an extensive complex, occupying a 200 acre site around which it will be possible to travel by tram. In attempting to recreate the pattern of life of a past society the planners aim to have an urban area with cobbled streets, shops, a post office and pub, a developed colliery area with nineteenth-century machinery and buildings, including pitmen's cottages, a horse-worked farm with a village on one side and a lead mine on the other, and various other essentials of full community life, such as a railway station, a chapel and a village school. It is also planned that steam engines will operate at specific times, and craftsmen will demonstrate their skills on the precincts. At the time of writing, some of the planning has already come to fruition, notably Rowley railway station, first built near Consett in 1867, a row of furnished cottages, and Home Farm with its old wooden horse wheel ('Gin-gan') fully restored to drive the threshing machine. Mobility throughout the site is provided by a former No. 10 Gateshead tramcar, which operates over that part of the track already laid. Altogether, the Beamish plan is probably the most exciting British development in many years, of museum presentation. When completed it will be a centre of living history that should enrich study at any level of the period with which it is concerned.

Castle Museum, York
Our third example, and the longest-established of the three, is the Castle Museum in York, a folk museum of Yorkshire domestic and social life from the seventeenth century onwards. It includes period rooms in Jacobean, Georgian and Victorian styles, as well as a one-roomed moorland cottage of the mid-nineteenth century. The galleries have a wide range of exhibits, including some renowned special collections, such as the period fireplaces and mantelpieces, each of which stands reconstructed as a separate unit complete with the appropriate hearth furniture, or the fire insurance marks which occupy one wall of the Chapel Gallery, or the arms and armour, reputedly one of the finest in the country. Costume, both military and civil, weights and measures, agricultural implements, toys, domestic lighting, valentines, musical instruments and a diversity of carved wooden articles are also represented. Elsewhere, a section of the museum (the cells of the old Debtors' Prison) has been converted into a series of reconstructed craft workshops—for comb making, clay pipe making, etc. The major attraction of this museum, however, is in its reconstructed streets, with rows of shop fronts, re-erected to help the visitor make the imaginative leap backwards into the past. Alderman's Walk, Kirkgate, Princess Mary Court and Half Moon Court are their names. To walk the length of the Kirkgate from the pewterer's and the copper shop at one end, past the apothecary's on the left, the coach house and fire station on the right, looking in turn into the toy shop, haberdashery, barber's and tobacconist's shops and a candle factory, is an experience which few youngsters can fail to enjoy. There is so much to savour and explore, not least

17

the latest addition of the Edwardian scene in Half Moon Court with the brilliantly reconstructed centre-piece of the King William IV Hotel in one corner. The imaginative presentation of the Museum's material is further enriched by the addition of a fully operating water-driven corn mill. In many ways the Castle Museum at York could with justification be regarded as a model and exemplar of everything that a good folk museum should be.

The examples chosen are numbered among the best of their kind that can be found. Many other folk museums are much simpler in respect of size and presentation. Nevertheless, their value for schools is very great in that they can tell much of the story of local heritage, background and traditions, and this can invariably be used either as a specific element in a local study, or as background to a broader theme which can be profitably extended by general reference to local contemporary life.

Finally, on the theme of folk museums, the point has already been made that, on account of their nature, one expects to find them sited in the locality to which their collections principally refer. One notable exception is the remarkable American Museum at Bath, an institution in no sense concerned with indigenous Anglo-Saxon or Celtic culture. Here, instead, one finds a folk museum translated from its native habitat and, through a series of galleries and furnished rooms, displaying American domestic life and decorative arts from the late seventeenth century to the mid-nineteenth. Famed not only for a first-rate collection of traditional museum exhibits but also for its American garden and the Washington gingerbread cooked in a genuine eighteenth-century oven, this delightful place has much to offer to any school whose history curriculum touches on the folk cultures of the United States of America.

By and large, the major contribution which the folk museum can make is towards the preservation of a community's sense of heritage. Perhaps one of the most surprising things about the pattern of British museums is that this has never been significantly fostered at a national level to the extent that one encounters it elsewhere. With the *Museu Artes Populares* at Lisbon, the Portuguese people have a rich treasure house of national costume, household articles and agricultural implements, gathered from all parts of the country. In the United States of America, the highly developed sense of the value of preserving the memory of the nation's past is nowhere better exemplified than in the capital's Smithsonian Institution, the superb complex of museums and art galleries that dominates the section of the Federal Mall lying to the east of the Washington Monument. Prominent among the elements that go to make up this finest of all American scientific and cultural institutions is the National Museum of History and Technology, much of which is given over to everyday life in the American past. In London's South Kensington complex we have something comparable to the Smithsonian, albeit on a much smaller scale, but the missing factor is undoubtedly the provision of a nationally focused folk museum. Nothing is more effective than this particular style of institution as a means of keeping alive the memory of how our forefathers lived and worked, and thereby fostering a sense of national pride and identity.

Like most oversimple classifications, the division into three categories—comprehensive, specialist, folk—is by no means a reliable guide to the nature of all the museums with which the school might properly be concerned. It is true that many museums will fall logically into one of those divisions. Nevertheless, not all small museums, with general collections of antiquities could, with justification, be lumped indiscriminately into the 'comprehensive' category, for some possess fairly strong groupings of exhibits on either the specialist or the folk side. For example, Anne of Cleves House in Lewes is an attractive half-timbered house which exhibits a collection of bygones—furniture, household equipment and costume. Within this it contains the John Every collection of ironwork and firebacks, items brought together by a former ironmaster and bequeathed on his death to the Sussex Archaeological Society. In this instance we have the example of a unique and comprehensive specialized collection existing within the main one. In the same way, the extensive Kelvingrove Museum and Art Gallery in Glasgow is as large a general collection as could be found in any of the major provincial cities of Britain. On the museum side its exhibits range over archaeology, history, ethnography, natural history, dress and technology; nevertheless, one of its major strengths lies in the inclusion within all this of the famous Scott Collection of arms and armour, a collection which in itself could furnish the essentials of a separate specialist museum.

The distinction between the specialist and the folk museum can also, in certain contexts, be blurred. Thus, while the Lewis Textile Museum at Blackburn is very much a specialist collection, with its seven-roomed presentation of the transition from domestic to factory-based industry, its location and the intimate association of the town with the growth and development of the textile industry would justify categorizing it as a centre of local folk study.

Sometimes one finds that the premises in which the museum is housed are an integral part of it. Bradford Industrial Museum, for example, is housed in an old textile mill. The main interest of the Rochdale Co-operative Museum, visited by co-operators from all over the world, stems from the fact that it is housed in the original premises, first opened as a store at Toad Lane in 1844. In the same way, the Castle Museum at York is located in two eighteenth-century prison buildings, the Debtors' Prison dating from 1705 and the Women's Prison dating from 1780, so that the outer fabric of the building, at least, is of direct relevance to any study of social life in York in the eighteenth century and is as much a part of the exhibited material as the items it contains. The fact that in this particular example the buildings are officially classified by the Department of the Environment demonstrates how broad categories like 'museum' and 'historical site' can often overlap.

Ship museums

In some cases a famous ship may be permanently preserved as a museum, and a number of those can be seen today, as lasting reminders of some significant episode or development in our national story. They are, in the main, specialist museums, and the most obvious example is probably that of HMS *Victory* at Portsmouth, nostalgically evocative of the great days of Nelson. London can boast of HMS *Discovery*, the ship on which Captain Scott journeyed in exploration to the Antarctic. The latest conversion is that of HMS *Belfast*, the largest cruiser ever built for the Royal Navy, now a permanent naval museum moored in the Thames, opposite to the Tower of London. At Greenwich the most famous of all clipper ships, *Cutty Sark*, is probably one of the best examples.

Visitors see the cargo hold where China tea and, later, Australian wool was stored and, beyond, in the bow of the ship, the desperately cramped quarters of the crew. When one stands on the quayside and notes the slim elegance, topped by the astonishingly complex mass of rigging, it is not difficult to conjure up in the mind's eye the picture of *Cutty Sark* in full sail, rounding the Horn in her efforts to be the first ship home from China with the new season's tea. To step on board such a vessel is to be transported back in time to another world. The work being currently undertaken at Bristol on Brunel's *Great Britain* will provide one more imaginative museum of this kind. It is regrettable that many similar opportunities are forfeited at the breaker's yard and, indeed, it is only thanks to the enterprise of the Californian Museum of the Sea Foundation that one of the most famous ships of all time has now, as the *Queen Mary* Museum, found a dignified resting place at the terminus of the Long Beach freeway in Los Angeles.

Finally, no conspectus of museum styles would be complete without reference to a remarkable experiment which has borne fruit at Coventry. This is the Lunt Fort, a timbered reconstruction of a large Roman fort, built by the methods employed by the Romans and patterned on evidence to be had from sources like Trajan's column. The latest addition is a timber granary, currently being equipped to house a Roman army museum.

Picture galleries

Before moving on to consider historical sites, there is one other type of location which has to be briefly considered, and that is the picture gallery. Strictly speaking, picture galleries are not museums, but in some respects their value as sources of historical reference is similar, in particular for the days before the invention of photography; they record the physical appearance and environment of men and women in times past. It is true that much art, particularly on the portrait side, tends to illuminate only the prosperous section of the community, nevertheless, the crisis of the Reformation implied some redirection of artistic skill, and this led, in part, to the emergence of the 'genre picture', the greatest exponenet of which was Brueghel, whose speciality was scenes from peasant life in the sixteenth century. His work has been described as a 'wealth of anecdote wit and observation'.[1] The example thus set by Brueghel was followed by generations of Flemish painters who explored to the full the possibilities of natural representation. Others have done the same— Canaletto, Renoir, Toulouse-Lautrec, Whistler, Van Gogh, Lowry— and have left us some of the finest possible historical documentation.

Historical sites

There are broad areas of overlap between museums and historical sites and, consequently, any attempt at definition is open to challenge. It may help if we begin by noting that one often finds a museum directly associated with a historical site. For example, the Roman site at Housesteads on Hadrian's Wall has, beside it, a small museum which houses some of the treasures which have been excavated, but which, by their nature, could not be left in the place where they were discovered without suffering erosion and ultimate destruction through exposure to the elements. In some cases, when the treasures are removed to the museum, replicas are left on the site, as at Tarxien in Malta, where the precious carved altar stones and the fertility godesses, fashioned originally from soft Maltese limestone, have been replaced by exact duplicates wrought in the same material. Sites of this kind, which have a museum in close relationship, are particularly valuable, in that they offer the fullest opportunity, not only for close inspection of the rare museum finds, but also for the forging of the imaginative link between the museum specimen and the environmental context to which it belongs.

Sometimes, of course, as previously mentioned, the functions are inextricably interwoven. At Carisbrooke Castle on the Isle of Wight schools have the complementary advantages of being able to visit a castle with medieval and Stuart connections as well as enjoy all the facilities which a well-run museum service has to offer in respect of intramural lecturing and the provision of worksheet and work book material. Nevertheless, the differentiation between the museum, and the historical site is fairly clear. If one accepts the simple distinction between the original site and some other place where treasures are displayed in a setting which is neither the original nor the natural habitat, the latter arrangement has the essentials of a museum struc-

[1] E. H. Gombrich, *The Story of Art*, Phaidon, 1972.

ture. In most instances, rather than leave the exhibits on the site, exposed to the dangers of deterioration or theft, it is infinitely better to rehouse them in a place specially designed to protect them. In some cases, of course, the object or objects may be too large, too permanent or too fragile to be moved, and other protective strategies need to be devised, as was done at Fishbourne, in the roofing over of the Roman mosaic pavements.

Generally speaking, therefore, the term 'historical site' may be held to encompass castles, churches, abbeys, cathedrals, battlefields, stately homes, town buildings such as guildhalls, almshouses, bridges, crosses, stocks, vennels, inns and any other such tangible survival from the fabric of our historical past. What, in essence, distinguishes historical sites from museums is that they are on original locations and may or may not have museum material associated with them.

One of the questions which is bound to be asked is about criteria for deciding when a particular place is or is not to be regarded as a historical site. Procedures for such decision-making have to a great extent been formalized by the Department of the Environment and other institutions, and are considered at greater length later in this chapter. Such procedures are probably the only rational way of tackling the job since on a broad philosophical definition almost everything would qualify, if only on the grounds that the shopping mall of today could well become the ancient monument of to-morrow; from this point of view, there is no valid historical justification for including in the 'historical site' category the medieval cathedral standing in a central location in town while at the same time excluding the parish church in the housing estate, built to conform to the architectural norms of the 1970s. Society in general, and historians in particular, would nevertheless make a distinction between two such ecclesiastical institutions, probably based on the antiquity of the cathedral, together with an appreciation of the events and personalities that featured in its past, elements which would go far towards guaranteeing a continuing respect for its future existence. By contrast, the modern parish church would be seen as a place which had made no such mark on the past, nor would it be seen to possess the rare quality of uniqueness that is a major part of the attraction of the older building.

Qualities such as antiquity, uniqueness, past importance in the life of a society, are all likely to affect the way in which we look at a place and the extent to which we are prepared to respect or even venerate it as a relic of the past. Not all such qualities will necessarily be present. For instance, much of our industrial archaeology material is not very old, but in the main, is likely to possess the other two features. This explains why the world's first iron bridge at Ironbridge and Abraham Darby's furnace at Coalbrookdale have together been preserved as the cherished nucleus of a major and growing complex, devoted to the historical origins of the Industrial Revolution in England.

All of this raises the issue of how survival can best be assured. Do we simply leave it to chance, to the operation of some national community psyche, which will somehow guarantee protection from the philistines? Or do we adopt formal procedures which will provide the machinery for securing the kind of legal protection that is the only certain safeguard? It is, in fact, the latter course which has, in particular, commended itself, so that well and not-so-well preserved Norman castles are likely to owe their continued existence to the fact that some official body or other group has made a point of securing at law those guarantees of their safety from the bulldozers of the speculative builders or the misplaced zeal of a local authority planning committee that wishes, perhaps, to place its new comprehensive school on the best site in town.

At this point it is appropriate to look briefly at the activities and services of three important agencies concerned with the protection and restoration of those places which are appropriately designated as of significance in relation to our national heritage. At the same time, it must not be assumed that everything that is protected necessarily comes under their care and supervision. Local authorities, small private groups, trusts of various kinds and private individuals are also widely concerned in the work of preservation. Nevertheless, a major part of it, and certainly the oversight of the most important historical sites, is undoubtedly the responsibility of three bodies.

Department of the Environment

This is the government department responsible in England for the preservation of what are termed 'ancient monuments' and 'historic buildings'. Since 1969 responsibility for such places in Scotland and

Wales has resided in the respective Secretaries of State, although executive work, and in particular the responsibility of carrying out expert restoration and similar services, still rests with the Department of the Environment.

The term 'ancient monument' has been given a fairly wide legislative definition and could be interpreted as applicable to almost any building or structure, dating from ancient to modern times, and deemed to be of historic interest. There are two notable exceptions. The first refers to ecclesiastical buildings in ecclesiastical use, so that cathedrals and churches that are still functional are excluded. The second exception is in respect of inhabited buildings. These, although not eligible for 'ancient monument' classification are protected by different legislation relative to what are termed 'historic buildings'. In this latter category, all buildings and structures dating from before 1700 are listed, as are most of those from between 1700 and 1840. From 1840 to 1914 there is a more limited selection of buildings 'of definite quality and character'. Listing has now begun on the period 1914—39, with selectivity criteria fairly strongly slanted towards buildings that are historically illustrative or demonstrate technological innovation, or those that have been associated with well-known characters or events. So, under one set of legislation the Department helps with the preservation of buildings which are still inhabited either as dwelling houses or for any other reason and which are regarded as of significance (e.g. industrial buildings, railway stations, markets, prisons, etc., seen as illustrative of social and economic history), whilst under another set it bears responsibility for the oversight of prehistoric earthworks, Roman villas, medieval castles, abbey remains, etc., all of which are grouped as 'ancient monuments'. For convenience, copies of the list of protected property are best consulted at local authority offices.

Having introduced the official classifications of 'ancient monument' and 'historic building', it might be as well to clarify the distinction between them and the term 'historical site', which is used throughout the present text. The first two are specifically definitive terms within the context of the work of the Department of the Environment. The description 'historical site' is one of the author's own choosing, generally applicable to all preserved places of historical interest that come under one of a number of possible controlling authorities, but, for reasons already considered, distinguished from museums. The term 'historical site' is therefore different in emphasis from those adopted as official terminology by the Department of the Environment and, although one would expect to find a considerable overlap in respect of what these different labels describe, they are not synonymous. A historic building in the care of the Department could be a historical site in the sense in which we are using the term, but it might, alternatively, be a museum.

At the time of writing (1976), the admission price for entry to places that come under the supervision of the Department of the Environment can vary from 5 to 80p. It is possible to purchase a season ticket, which gives unlimited entry at a cost of £2 per annum; for children under sixteen and old-age pensioners the price is 75p. Obviously, for a person wishing to make any kind of regular use of the monuments or buildings these rates are very favourable. Teachers requiring to prepare work material and, in the process, likely to be involved in making a recurrent number of visits to a particular place, would do well to consider the advantages which such a concession can offer. The additional value, for recreation and vacation times, of having a season ticket of this kind will be obvious.

Apart from season ticket entry, there are special arrangements which allow for the free admission of certain categories of parties engaged in educational visits. These cover school groups, or groups of students taking full-time courses at establishments of further education, including colleges of education and central institutions. The facilities do not extend to youth or other organizations. In respect of free admission, two schemes, which have been subject to very recent revision, are currently in operation.

The first is known as the Permit scheme, and its purpose is to cater for parties of pupils or students wishing to make occasional weekday visits to ancient monuments and historic buildings, situated at some distance from the school or college concerned. Application should be made on Department of the Environment Form AM 24, stocks of which ought to be held by employing authorities of schools or colleges. Teachers who find otherwise can obtain them direct from the Department's regional office. Permits are issued for one date only and a maximum of 100 pupils or students are admitted daily from any one educational establishment. There is, in addition, an upper limit, variable according to the nature of the site, to the total number of free admissions made up from all visiting groups on any one day, so that, in the event of the quota being used up, a school or college making application may be offered an alternative date. It is not possible to have a permit issued for a Sunday or a holiday time, e.g. Easter Saturday, and during the summer months on certain sites such as the Tower of London, Hampton Court Palace, Stonehenge and Edinburgh Castle, the permit system is suspended. On all visits, the Department, rightly, insists on the school or college making adequate provision for the supervision of the visiting group and lays down a basic ratio of one member of school or college staff to each fifteen pupils or students (raised to one in twelve in the case of Edinburgh Castle). Permit applications have to be made to the Department of the Environment by the employing authority or by the teaching institution itself, at least ten days in advance of a visit.

The alternative is the Student Ticket scheme, and its aim is to provide for similar groups to make frequent visits to monuments and historic buildings that lie within easily accessible reach of the school and college. In this case the education authorities have custody of group admission tickets and the school or college draws them on loan when required. Restrictions on times when they can be used are similar to those applying to the Permit scheme. The system operates on the basis of six student group tickets being available for each of the monuments and historic buildings in the care of the Secretaries of State. There are certain important exceptions to it, for the scheme does not apply to the three castles of Caernarvon, Carisbrooke and Dover, nor to the monuments and historic buildings in Greater London. For certain other sites, such as Fountain's Abbey, Porchester Castle, Stonehenge, the system is suspended during the summer months. Each ticket admits a party of up to fifty pupils or students, and there must be at least one supervising member of staff to every other fifteen members of the group. Education authorities apply for tickets and, if available, these are issued. The tickets are fully transferable, so that an authority whose requests have not been met in full, may arrange to make up its required number by borrowing from a neighbouring authority. Such arrangements, of course, can be reciprocal. In Scotland the scheme has been discontinued, except for the Orkney, Shetland and Western Isles.

The National Trust

Contrary to what the name would suggest, this is not an official government agency, but a charitable organization. When incorporated as a trust in 1907, its original mandate by Act of Parliament was, 'to promote the permanent preservation for the benefit of the nation of land and buildings of beauty or historic interest'. Dependent as it has been since its inception on the contributions of donors, subscriptions of members and entry fees paid by the public, it has maintained its charge with great distinction. The National Trust operates in England, Wales and Northern Ireland and, in its concern for the preservation of the natural beauty of the countryside, it has acquired no less than 45,000 acres. In the process, it has outstripped both the Crown and the Church to become the largest private landholder in the United Kingdom. Included in its properties are seventeen villages (e.g. Lacock, West Wycombe), famous gardens, farms, windmills, watermills, historic antiquities (including a part of Hadrian's Wall), bird sanctuaries, lakes, hills, including the Neolithic causewayed enclosure of Windmill Hill, canals, bridges and more than 200 buildings of architectural or historic significance. All these it makes available to visiting members of the public. Many are great country houses which, in consequence of the support of the Trust in preservation and maintenance, can still be inhabited. A number of the Trust's possessions are houses in which great men and women— Wordsworth, Coleridge, Kipling, Thomas Hardy, Lawrence of Arabia, Beatrix Potter, Bernard Shaw, Ellen Terry, Thomas Carlyle, Sir Winston Churchill—lived and worked.

Enough has probably been said for it to be appreciated that without the activity of the National Trust, much that has survived of our heritage from the past would have long since disappeared. The care and upkeep of the antiquities which are in trusteeship depends on several things, in particular the nature and location of the site and the amount of funds available. A small number which are of major importance are looked after on behalf of the Trust by the Department of the Environment, and some are in the care of the Nature Conservancy. Others are maintained in consequence of generous grants from local authorities and elsewhere. In the case of the rest, the National Trust has to see to their upkeep entirely from its own resources including, not least, voluntary help in keeping sites tidy and preventing them from becoming overgrown.

For schools, colleges or youth organizations, the Junior corporate membership scheme is particularly recommended. The annual cost is £10 and a group membership card entitles two leaders and a maximum of thirty pupils or students under twenty-one years of age to visit any property of the National Trust free of charge. The group also receives Trust publications and invitations to its meetings. The Trust's Junior Division arranges lectures and film shows on various aspects of National Trust work, and is responsible for the provision of information on its historic houses and other protected property. Individual membership is at an annual rate of £5 for adults or £2 for all those under twenty-one. Family membership is offered at £5 for the first member, and £2 for each additional one. Membership, whether group or individual, also allows free entry into the properties controlled by the National Trust for Scotland, which is a separate organization.

The National Trust for Scotland

Its activities are broadly similar to those of the National Trust, although the problems of conservation which it is now having to face are probably much more serious than anything with which its sister organization has ever had to cope. This stems from the discovery of offshore oil and gas resources, and the consequent resolve of the National Trust for Scotland to impress on central government the desirability of ensuring that planning strategies should be conducted in such a way as to ensure the maximum compatibility with what is already there.

The National Trust for Scotland has also a wide range of protected properties, although on a smaller scale than that of the National Trust. Castles and country houses are well represented, as are smaller houses, such as Gladstone Land in Edinburgh or Provost Ross's House in Aberdeen. Gardens, mountainous country (e.g. Glencoe), islands and waterfalls are included, as well as historic sites, such as the battlefields of Bannockburn, Culloden and Killiecrankie. Like the National Trust, the organization has also concerned itself with the preservation of property associated with famous people, and included in this category are the birthplaces of J. M. Barrie and Thomas Carlyle. Upkeep of property is generally financed by the Trust but, as in the case of the English-based counterpart, some particularly important sites are also under the guardianship of the Department of the Environment. This includes such places as the Roman Wall at Falkirk and the 'Palace' at Culross in Fife.

Membership arrangements are little different from those of the National Trust. Corporate membership operates similarly on the basis of an annual £10 fee. Ordinary adult membership is £5, and Junior membership is also £2 per annum, with an upper age limit of twenty-one. Family membership is £8 per annum. There is a reciprocal arrangement to the one offered by the sister organization, in that those holding membership of the National Trust for Scotland may also be admitted free to properties of the National Trust in England, Wales and Northern Ireland.

The purpose of this brief review of museums, historical sites and their controlling authorities has been to try to look in a logical way at what is available. The exercise of categorizing museums and other places is not in itself intrinsically important, but it does help with the process of identifying the types that, in varying circumstances, are most likely to be of value to schools. Once a teacher has started to think about the nature of the local museums, he or she has gone far towards coming to terms with the ways in which they can best serve the pupils' needs.

It is hoped that sufficient has been said to highlight the changes that have taken place, particularly in museums. Many of them are very different places today from those of a generation ago. If such trends continue, we are likely to find them increasingly useful and relevant to historical studies, repositories of some of the most precious remains of the past, and focuses of permanent inspiration for the young. To design history courses so as to bring pupils into direct contact with the physical remnants of past ages is to move imperceptibly closer towards making the past come alive, if only briefly. Museums are not, and never were, dead places, however unimaginative the layout of their contents. Nowadays, the opportunities are probably better than ever before for the fostering of an interest in past cultures, and for bringing us to an awareness of how the surviving physical remains of the past can help the child to understand much of his present life-style and habits. It is true that some schools are in a better position than others for tapping such resources; Leicestershire, for example, is particularly strong on local museums. Certain schools are also favourably placed to take advantage of the special exhibitions staged by major museum centres; schools in the London area, for example, have relatively easy access to the outstanding presentations mounted by the British Museum. These can vary from studies of Grime's Graves and the British flint miners, to displays of Egyptian literacy or English Restoration bookbindings. Nevertheless, electrified train services are now making it possible for many more school parties to travel much longer distances. One of the most outstanding demonstrations of the fact that distance is not always regarded as an impediment was the enthusiastic response from schools all over the country to the splendid 'Treasures of Tutankhamun' exhibition of 1972.

Safety and control

No consideration of visiting historical sites would be complete without a mention of the need for care and safety. More than one reference has already been made to the desirability of adequate supervision of children during outside visits; nor must one regard as an irritating formality the insistence of the Department of the Environment and bodies like the National Trust, upon a defined ratio of staff and pupils. It is one thing to leave children in peace to get on with a set task. Indeed, the wise teacher knows when intrusion is undesirable and, in refraining from it, is simply exercising his professional skill. It is quite a different matter to relinquish control and allow behaviour that can be antisocial, or even possibly dangerous to the visitors themselves. Prehistoric earthworks, for example, are often characterized by mounds, slopes and gullies, and a slide down is an activity that might well tempt the young visitor. There are instances where the disfiguring consequences of this kind of action, when repeated over a period of time, can be destructive of the site itself. For the same reason, teachers must not allow or encourage any kind of amateur archaeological investigation, for this can be very harmful. It is because of this that the National Trust is so vigilant about protecting its property from the depredations of archaeologists, professional and amateur alike, so that, except in very special instances, permission to excavate is never given.

As regards safety, one has only to look over the low ramparts of Edinburgh Castle and down the sheer face of the rock on which it is set to realize why the Department of the Environment insists here upon the highest ratio of supervision of all its sites: one member of staff to each twelve pupils or students. Most supervised sites have adequate protection against accidents, but no place is proof against anyone who is determined to behave foolishly in the face of potential danger.

3

Organizing the Visit

In considering the nature of museum or field study visits, it has to be recognized that these vary enormously in respect of the demands made on the teacher. At one end of the scale, there is the simple short outing of, perhaps, no more than an hour's duration to some venue in the immediate locality of the school. The excursion of a week or more's duration to a far-away place obviously presents a much greater challenge to the teacher's administrative and organizational skill. Between those two widely differing situations lies a whole range of alternative possibilities.

In a general text of this kind, no more than a passing mention can be given to study tours of an extensive nature. Teachers of ambition and resource who wish to undertake such ventures will have to face greater problems, in the way of providing food, accommodation, and transport arrangements than those which arise for run-of-the-mill school excursions. It is true that, on occasions, school parties do go to Moscow, Istanbul and New York, but such trips are exceptional and outside the scope of this book. Teachers embarking on extra-mural studies of the kind envisaged here are more likely to be involved in the organization of full-day or part-day outings and it is with the preliminaries for these that the present chapter is especially concerned.

Most teachers who have experience of arranging outings of this kind would probably concede that the initial stage of preparation is of far greater importance than is commonly acknowledged. Time and again it is demonstrated that whatever is hoped for in the way of educational gains depends to a considerable extent on the thoroughness and skill which the teacher is able to bring to bear upon the preliminary arrangements.

There are two aspects of preparation which require detailed consideration. One is concerned with the compilation of work material for pupils, the other with essential administrative preparation. Work material related to the study theme is the teacher's main professional care. The administrative arrangements are not primarily directed towards educational objectives, yet they are essential if the outing is to be successful in achieving its purpose. For this reason, it is proposed to deal with the preparation of work material in Chapters 4 and 5, and to confine this chapter to matters of preliminary administration.

In the organization of any such outing as is envisaged, certain essential tasks can be distinguished and these may now be considered in what would probably be their approximate order of disposal.

Establishment of the nature of the authority in charge

The first thing to be clarified is the controlling authority of the particular museum or site which is the object of the visit. This could be one of a number of possibilities, such as:

Department of the Environment
National Trust
National Trust for Scotland
Regional or local authority
Private (e.g. individual, trust, society).

This information is fairly easy to come by, and details of the first three on the above list have been given in the previous chapter. For general information, there is a good informative guide entitled *The Guide to Stately Homes, Castles and Gardens*, published by the Automobile Association. Drive Publications have also recently updated their excellent *Treasures of Britain*, which is a beautifully illustrated book, with good supporting maps. Specifically on museums, one of the most useful guides is *Museums and Galleries in Great Britain and Ireland*, an annual publication. Cross-indexing is a feature of its design, and most museums are represented. It is published by ABC Travel Guides Ltd, Old Hill, London Road, Dunstable LU6 3EB, and is available either from the publisher or from leading newsagents. Some of the bigger museums carry copies on their sales stalls.

Contact with the curator or custodian

Once the nature of the controlling authority is established, the next step is to make an initial contact, either by letter or by personal visit. At this stage the person in charge of the museum or site should be notified of three things: the timing of the visit, the degree of help needed and the composition of the party.

The date and time of the proposed visit

Informing a curator or custodian of this is a matter of courtesy. It is true that many museums and sites are regularly open to the public and that there is no question of having to make appointments to view; nevertheless, the casual incursion of individuals or family groups is a very different matter from the unannounced 'invasion' of forty to fifty children, accompanied by a teacher whose degree of organizational skill or whose strength of control in handling the group may be taxed to its limit. Many museum curators will testify to the havoc which can be created by groups that are too loosely organized and perhaps insufficiently guided in order to ensure optimum results from the visit. Museums and other places therefore like to be informed of a school's intention to bring along a sizeable party in order that any necessary assistance to the teacher can be discussed or determined in advance. Forethought of this kind will invariably go far towards making the visit a success, as well as smoothing future relationships.

There is another very good reason for notifying the curator or custodian of the date and time of the proposed visit, and that is to ensure that the museum or site will be open when the party arrives. The information is usually obtainable from the appropriate printed sources (for example, the two guide books mentioned above); all the same, it is advisable to check, because the permanency of declared opening times can never be assumed. Besides, it is advisable to safeguard against the possibility that the particular section which one proposes to use may be temporarily closed due to rearrangement of exhibits or redecoration of the rooms, or even, perhaps, because some other group has booked the exclusive use of it. The possibility too, that the mounting of a special exhibition may have led to the temporary closure, displacement or removal of regularly displayed exhibits must not be overlooked.

In this connection, the writer well recollects the experience which a colleague had some years ago. The objective of the intended visit was a fifteenth-century house which contained a collection of domestic articles and was situated near the old medieval town centre of Glasgow; the group concerned consisted of approximately two dozen young ladies in the final year of their teacher-training course. It being fairly common knowledge that the proposed venue was open from ten to five throughout the week, the party set off in good heart one Thursday afternoon and arrived by public transport at the house. Only then did they discover that although the hearsay information about opening times was correct, it was subject to the qualification that the museum was closed to the public on Thursday afternoons. This was something which had not been anticipated, but the tutor was a man of some resource, and, after making an eloquent apology to the party, he hastened to point out that as the medieval cathedral of St Mungo was but 200 yards away across the square, it was only a question of redirecting the object of the visit. It being agreed that this would be not only a rational course but also an educationally respectable one, the little party set off towards their new objective. Fate, however, had determined that on this particular afternoon there could be no conducted tours of the cathedral, a fact apparent to the group almost as soon as they had drawn near enough to be able to perceive a sizeable body of wedding guests arriving at the west door. The tutor later admitted to having felt not a mite nonplussed at the rapidity with which he appeared to be running out of ancient monuments, but, being a gentleman with substantial reserves of initiative, he quickly redeployed his group through the nave and into the rear choir stalls. Within minutes, all were standing to sing 'Oh perfect love', a sentiment which, however admirable, did not really impinge with any direct relevance upon the original plan of the visit. Ironically, of course, the sequel was that the young ladies were unanimous in acclaiming it as the best-ever afternoon in a college course that had lasted for almost three years! Fortune had in the end shone upon the fair, but it was only too apparent how close to disaster the whole outing had been.

The extent to which help is required
Some museums and many historical sites offer the services of guides.

Some of these are very good and, as an outstanding example, one might point to the provision made at the Victoria and Albert Museum. The British Museum (Natural History) in Cromwell Road, London, is another particularly good example of a place where the need for guided tours has been met by employing 'auxiliaries' who have been trained at the Museum and are especially competent to conduct parties round the galleries for something like an hour's session. The same high professional standard is encountered elsewhere, but one does still have to beware of situations where guides are either tedious or else prepared only to offer set commentaries full of indisputably entertaining diversion and dubious folk-lore, but too often deficient in educational quality. Happily, with the spread of professionalism in the museum service, they are tending to disappear, so that, for the most part, one is now likely to hear well informed and well presented material. Where the museum has developed this kind of guidance to a high standard, the teacher should take advantage of the opportunities offered, particularly in situations where children are being introduced to the place for the first time. The Roman bath site at Bath, which offers the services of skilled guides who are also able to employ the most sophisticated of presentation techniques, is a good example. In the darkness of the excavated area there is an elaborate lighting system designed to allow the skilled commentator to illuminate one, two or more sections of the excavations at a time, in order to keep pace with the talk.

Guided tours, of course, may often be supplied by a museum on a self-directional basis. To an increasing extent museums and sites have been providing hiring facilities in the form of transistorized audioguides. Here, for example, is the introduction to a Soundguide tour of Fountains Hall:

You are now standing in the Stone Hall of Fountains Hall. It's a Hall that we shall be getting a dramatic glimpse of on our way round and to which we shall return at the end of our tour. For the moment we are just using it as a starting point—as a place where we can try out our Soundguide machine.

You have already used the on and off lever, and you can control the level of my voice by turning the little wheel just below the lever. Try it for yourself.

Now I want you to go out of this room through the door opposite the one

37

you came in by and turn right and right again. You will then be entering a passage at the end of which is a bedroom. Switch on again when you are in that bedroom, but switch off now.

(*Switch pause*)

This is the best bedroom, and the first thing that strikes one is the bed, or possibly not so much the bed as the deep rose brocade that covers it and almost overwhelms it. This bed actually came from another house nearby— Studley Royal. And when it was at Studley Royal it was slept in by three reigning queens—Queen Alexandra, Queen Mary, and Elizabeth, the Queen to George the sixth.

The portrait of three children over the fireplace shows us . . .

It will be appreciated that there is a limit to the desirability of technological aid in such a situation. It is manifestly beneficial to use an audio-guide, which engages only the aural senses, but advantageously leaves the eyes free to look at what should be examined. By the same argument, its extension, within the museum or site, into the form of a tape-slide presentation is likely to be irrelevant and distracting, and yet there are instances where such misapplied technology is found. Again, it is worth reflecting that the audio-aid is only a sophisticated, albeit in some ways more convenient, version of what could just as easily be given on paper, again provided that the amount of reading was not so excessive as to leave the student with too little time for looking at the exhibits.

For a school party the principal advantage of the guided tour, self-directional or otherwise, is that it is a very useful way of introducing a museum or site. Tightly structured work directives, which usually focus attention on a predetermined set of exhibits, have a particular relevance in the context of a project study. In situations, however, where the school group is, perhaps, visiting the museum for the first time and there is no desire on the part of the teacher to direct attention towards any special object or group of objects, the general guided tour, whether in an audio-recorded form or as a printed study guide, is a perfectly acceptable alternative.

Quite apart from the provision of work directives or of the simple tour guide, many major museums offer, within the galleries, lessons on a wide variety of subjects, making use of exhibits in conjunction with an extensive range of audio-visual resources, and so presenting material at the highest level of professional expertise. Tour guides, work directives and other museum-based services are considered in greater detail in later chapters. The point to be made at this stage is that, whatever the nature of the services on offer by the museum or site, the teacher must still decide in advance whether or not he wishes to use them, in whole or in part, and, having decided, must inform the custodian accordingly. If the teacher's intention is to handle the visit himself and have the children work from school-produced directives, it does much for public relations if this is made clear in the preliminary correspondence. If at the same time the teacher can with confidence offer reassurance to the curator that school parties will be properly supervised during the visit, much will have been done to promote harmonious relationships.

The number in the party

The custodian should be notified in advance of the intended size of the party, in respect of both adults and children; the age of the pupils should also be indicated. This is particularly important if the museum or site is a small one. The general point regarding courtesy has already been made. There are, however, other reasons why it is desirable to supply the custodian with such information, in order to obviate the less desirable consequences of a surprise visit with a large group. An overcrowded museum is undesirable, as much from the point of view of the visitors as from that of the staff. This is why some of the more popular places operate a booking system for school parties, so that they can avoid the inconvenience of having too many groups in at the same time. Sometimes, of course, it is unavoidable but preliminary consultation provides an opportunity for considering possible alternative dates. In some instances, too, there might be a restriction upon numbers. This could be absolute, as in the case, perhaps, of permission to visit a historic house, privately owned, or it might mean the division of the main party into smaller groups, for example in the case of a visit to the Royal Mint or the Jewellery Gallery of the Victoria and Albert Museum. Whatever the nature, it is desirable to know in advance of any special conditions required by the museum or site.

One advantage in providing the museum or site with details of the number in the party is that it may lead to a reduction in admission costs. Many places allow free admissions but there are others where an entry fee is charged, and it is often possible to have this reduced for a party. Such arrangements vary a great deal, especially where private ownership is involved. If the museum or site is controlled by the Department of the Environment, special concession entry can be obtained, according to the procedures outlined in the previous chapter.

As a final observation on this point, it should be noted that some places anticipate the need to have this detailed information from schools and provide a form for the purpose, to be completed and submitted by the teacher organizing the future visit. You can see an example of this in the Ironbridge Gorge Museum Trust booking form shown here.

Ironbridge Gorge Museum Trust

Party bookings

If you are bringing a party of people to the Ironbridge Gorge Museum you can help us ensure that your visit runs smoothly by completing and posting the attached booking form.

Coalbrookdale Museum & Furnace Site and Blists Hill Open Air Museum are both open daily from 10.00 to 18.00, April to October inclusive.

Your party may visit both in the same day but allow at least an hour for Coalbrookdale and two hours to get around Blists Hill. You can make either of them your first port of call. You may also plan to spend half an hour at each of the Iron Bridge, Tar Tunnel and Bedlam Furnaces.

Guide services can be booked. The charge is £3 per session.

Admission	Adults	Children 15 and under
Coalbrookdale	20p	10p
Blists Hill	20p	10p
Combined ticket, Coalbrookdale and Blists Hill	30p	15p
Tar Tunnel	10p	5p

Old age pensioners and students in full time education are admitted at half the adult price.

Car park free

If you are bringing children please make sure that there is at least one adult in the party for every 25 children.

A Museum publications list is enclosed and any order placed for your party will be dealt with by return of post.

To
Ironbridge Gorge Museum Trust,
Church Hill, Ironbridge, Telford, Shropshire, TF8 7RE.

Party booking

Name of party ....

....

Number in party ....

Date preferred for visit ....

....

Acceptable alternatives ....

....

Proposed times of arrival:

Coalbrookdale ....

Blists Hill ....

Tar Tunnel ....

Please complete expected time of arrival at each site. You may visit the sites in any order and need not, of course, see them all during one visit.

Guide required

    Blists Hill : YES/NO

Coalbrookdale : YES/NO

Signature of organizer ....

Date ....

Address ....

....

....

....

Telephone number ....

Party booking form, Ironbridge Gorge Museum Trust

Knowledge of the route

Getting the party to its objective is something which has to be thought about. It may be that, as far as the teacher is concerned, this is not a major responsibility. In the case of local visits, there may be no transport involved at all. In others, even where the party is going further afield, if public transport is used the problem resolves itself into one of organizing movement at the terminal points, and, in particular, knowing where to get off and which road to take thereafter. In this way, for example, a group of children could be taken most of the way from Chigwell to the British Museum by the Central Line of the London underground system. Once on the way, the teacher's responsibility in this respect would be limited to escorting the pupils off the train at Holborn, and conducting them to Great Russell Street via Bloomsbury Square.

There are, however, situations when full responsibility for navigating the entire outing rests fairly and squarely with the person in charge. Of such a kind are road journeys by hired coach, and it is imperative that the teacher should be familiar in advance with the route. There is only one completely satisfactory way to ensure this, and that is to undertake a preliminary personal reconnaissance, preferably with a reliable road atlas. To omit to do this is to invite possible disaster. So, on the assumption that the teacher has both time and opportunity to carry out such an essential preliminary, the following features could, in particular, be noted.

Road signs

There may be points where the road signs are insufficiently clear and where there is a possibility of losing the way. British road signposting varies markedly from area to area and it is possible, especially on the secondary roads, to find many places where no clue is given and where the right decision is dependent on chance or map reading. Since it is the teacher who has to guide the driver, proper foreknowledge with regard to hazards, such as unmarked T junctions, is highly desirable.

Parking places

The position of parking places must also be thought out in advance and the choice examined in the light of what is possible and what allowed. The possibility that the bus driver will be familiar with the parking regulations in a relatively obscure town whose attraction is its fifteenth-century church cannot be assumed, even if the hiring company's offices are located within a relatively short distance of it. A driver fully aware of arrangements at neighbouring football grounds, may be less sure in respect of places of historic interest.

The location of public lavatories

Particularly on a school outing, it is very useful not only to know precisely where lavatories are to be found—on the route as well as at the destination—but also if they are open. To those who have never experienced the situation, it may seem incomprehensible to learn that, for a number of reasons, some local authorities actually lock them up at a certain hour, and others keep them closed all day on Sundays.

Access by coach

Points relatively easy of access by private car can sometimes be very difficult to reach by coach. A number of places in Cornwall qualify for inclusion in this category. Scotland, too, has a fair sprinkling of such locations. For example, the village of Culross in Fife, many of whose treasured buildings are under the protection of the National Trust for Scotland, can be approached by car on either the high road or the coast road. The fact that there is a very steep hill down to the village from the top road makes the coast route the only practical possibility for coaches.

Where teachers, in consequences of professional commitment, are precluded from undertaking this preliminary scout around, familiarization must be undertaken vicariously, by means of a good, up-to-date road atlas. This is very much a second-best procedure and will provide no guarantee that the teacher is adequately informed. Nevertheless, it is better than setting out blind and, in certain circumstances, can be an adequate substitute for a personal preliminary visit.

Transport arrangements

Ideally transport should be arranged well in advance. There are a number of possibilities and choice will be determined largely by the criteria of cost and convenience.

Travel by road

Very small groups can be transported by one or two private cars, although if this is done, particular attention must be paid to the matter of insurance (see below). However, for school parties, travel by ordinary service transport is probably more usual in situations where the number of pupils is few and manageable. In this way, a group of anything up to a dozen pupils from a Leicester city school, wishing to view the church or museum at Melton Mowbray, would logically take the local bus (No. 630). In many other instances, the number will often be sufficiently large, or the destination so difficult of access, to warrant the hire of a coach from a local bus company. Such firms are numerous and a school may find it advantageous to have a regular arrangement with one such firm. This can bring attendant advantages in respect of hiring fee concessions, and drivers may also become accustomed to the routine of a planned historical outing as well as gaining familiarity with the commoner routes selected for day excursions.

It is worth noting that most private hirers of this kind charge for the coach, without regard to whether or not all seats are occupied. In view of this, it is advisable to book whichever bus is most economical in size, but it needs to be borne in mind that certain economies in this direction can be false ones, and specially if they are achieved at the expense of the comfort of the travellers. For example, if thirty-two people are involved and the company can offer for hire either a thirty-seater or a forty-seater coach, then it might well be tempting, on grounds of economy, to go for the smaller of the two vehicles. On the other hand, the overriding disadvantage of such a decision lies in the fact that, at two points on the bus, three children would require to be allocated to a seat designed to accommodate two; as any experienced teacher will confirm, this is asking for trouble, in more ways than one! In such circumstances, it would be better to go for the forty-seater and, if necessary, find extra individuals to fill up some, at least, of the empty spaces available.

Travel by rail

Concession bookings for parties are from time to time available from British Rail, and these are especially valuable for local journeys.

In the case of the longer journey, terms tend on the whole to be less advantageous, although certain recently introduced day return fares on some inter-city routes are offered at highly advantageous rates.

By contrast with coach travel, one principal advantage of journeying by train is speed—something like half the time in many cases. On the other hand, there is much less flexibility, and a group could be faced with a considerable walk to and from the station at each end of the journey. Supplementary transport can be arranged to overcome the problem, but this can complicate the arrangements as well as introduce an added risk of something going wrong. In general, the school's location in relation to the railway station, and the corresponding situation of the place to be visited will be the principal determining factors as between rail or coach. Schools in the London area are particularly fortunate in being able to use the underground system, and it is a reassuringly common sight to see the Bakerloo line regularly justifying its educational function by the daily disgorging at Lambeth North of classes of schoolchildren heading for that most popular of venues, the Imperial War Museum.

Travel by air

In these days of higher fuel costs and declining airline fortunes, it is perhaps superfluous and somewhat unrealistic to speak of air travel. Nevertheless, charter flights for educational purposes are still, if not common, certainly being undertaken. There are still airlines which will deal sympathetically with requests for special rates, especially if they are made at a time of the year well outside of the limits of the holiday season. But it would probably be true to say that this extremely expensive type of transport could only justify itself if its principal purpose were educational and the intention were to do something which could not be achieved by alternative means. An air journey would hardly be warranted if undertaken simply on grounds of mobility and convenience, but if it were to be an integral part of a historical, geographical and economic study of the Thames Valley, then it could at least be upheld as intrinsically valuable when measured in terms of educational outcomes.

Staff duties

For a number of reasons, adequate staffing is an absolute necessity on any school outing. A ratio of one teacher to twenty pupils could be taken as a general recommendation, subject to any special conditions. The apportionment of duties among members of staff has to be thought out in advance, and it is advisable to make explicit where individual and particular responsibilities are to lie. If more than one member of staff is to be charged with undertaking a particular duty, then it is equally necessary to make clear who has overall charge. In the case of a whole-day outing by coach, responsibility probably needs to be assigned for a number of particular jobs, such as:

- collection and custody of a first-aid box
- catering (if any)
- provision of a large cardboard carton for litter
- distribution and custody of clip boards, pencils, worksheets
- general supervision of children at the museum or on the site
- counting of heads before each coach departure
- any other particular duties which emerge from the specific nature of the visit.

Insurance

Teachers entrusted with the responsibility of looking after children out of school hours should never overlook the simple precaution of seeing that the party is adequately insured. For example, in the case of a small group taken on a visit in one or two private cars, the insurance, even in the case of a so-called 'comprehensive' policy, may not cover the passengers for personal injury, so that the onus of responsibility lies on the car owner to provide proper cover. It is for this reason that motoring organizations warn their members to be careful about giving lifts, especially when public transport is not readily available.

In the case of larger parties using coach hire transport it may be imagined that this problem is no longer applicable. Yet even in such circumstances, it cannot be assumed that insurance cover for passengers is automatic. Some bus companies neither do it, nor make clear that they do not do it, and it is advisable to enquire whether or not the employing education authority has any standing arrangements for insurance. It may, for example, be in the habit of doing business with one particular company or group of companies, from which it perhaps receives special rates. Whatever the circumstances, short period personal cover is very simple to arrange and almost any insurance company will offer it at a small sum per head for an afternoon or day outing. All the teacher has to do is to contact a company (if the local authority does not wish to advise on this, then the Yellow Pages of the telephone directory should provide an adequate guide), submit their completed form a few weeks before the time of the outing and, once accepted, pay the premium required.

Parental permission

It is always advisable to secure parental agreement, even in the case of a half-day outing, and the fact that such permission may on occasions be withheld is all the more reason for establishing the practice as a regular procedure. Securing it can be achieved by asking the parent to sign a simple clearance slip, which ought to have on it details of the date, time and place to be visited. This ensures that the parent is kept fully informed and, in cases where the visit is likely to be so extended as to mean that children would be returning home a little later than the normal time, it can also be used to communicate such information and thus allay in advance any worry that might otherwise arise.

Some authorities include in the clearance slip a declaration that the parent will not hold the school responsible for injury or loss sustained by the pupil. This is a wise addition, and teachers should not shrink from including it. Some schools or employing authorities have a set form to cover this, but if not, and if the teacher is in any doubt as how to frame such a declaration, one or other of the teachers' organizations should be consulted and should be able to provide the correct advice. It must, of course, be clearly understood that the purpose of securing a parental signature to a document of this kind is not to absolve the teacher from the legal and moral responsibilities which he or she has for taking all possible care for the safety and welfare of the pupils. It would be both naïve and irresponsible to imagine that it could ever do this. On the other hand, it may be some kind of safeguard against frivolous claims, founded on the mistaken notion that the teacher's responsibilities are in some way all-encompassing and that it is a part of his task always to ensure that Willie remembers to pick up his bag before leaving the museum. In short, for the teacher it is no defence against negligence but may cushion him against unreasonable claims.

Time allocation

The working out of a time schedule, both for the journey and for the places to be visited, is a necessary part of the preparation. The elements are probably best considered in the following order:

1. Times of departure and return
2. Estimated duration of journey
3. Length of time to be spent on visits
4. Free time.

Estimation of the journey time, in relation to total time available will show fairly clearly how much is left for the real purpose of the outing. If this simple calculation reveals that insufficient time is available then, clearly, the plan for the day is over-ambitious and consideration may have to be given to leaving something out. If it appears that the amount of time left over after the deduction of journey time is excessive in relation to the chosen goals, it may well be worth considering the possibility of extending the programme by the inclusion of an additional relevant item.

Reckoning of rail journey time can usually be fairly accurate, but if the intention is to travel by unscheduled coach, then assessment of time required may vary considerably according to the nature of the roads. For example, one could take a party from north London to Coventry in about two-and-a-half hours, because for most of the way the group would be travelling on motorway. Conversely, a journey undertaken on an ordinary two-way traffic highway, running through the centre of towns and villages, would take very much longer. In the latter circumstances, it would probably be in order, allowing for stops and the generally lower rate of travelling speed, to assume a basis of 25−30 m.p.h. as the probable average speed of the coach.

Time spent in the sites or museums should always be adequate, or there is no point in going at all. On the matter of allowing the children a certain amount of free time, it is for the teacher to decide the extent to which this would be appropriate. If it is understood that free time is to be allowed, then it must be worked into the programme.

Whatever has been said up to now on the matter of planning, flexibility should still be retained. This means that one ought to be prepared to make alterations, because emergencies frequently occur. Furthermore, a place can sometimes turn out to have more of interest in it than had been anticipated. Nevertheless, if on-the-spot changes do have to be made, then the existence of a carefully thought-out schedule can be a useful basis for emergency planning. Far from inhibiting the decision-making in any way, it can be a positive help, in that the overall picture it presents enables the group organizer to see at a glance which items in the programme can be extended or limited or, perhaps, dispensed with altogether, according to the nature of the new situation.

Finally, it is worth bearing in mind (and this would apply at all stages of the outing) that it is always preferable to overestimate rather than to allow too little time; it never does any harm to have a little in reserve, to cope with the unexpected.

Estimation of expense

It is advisable to estimate expense at a fairly early stage in the proceedings. To the cost of the transport should be added any entry fees and cloakroom charges. Allowance should also be made for possible gratuities, especially perhaps in the case of coach drivers and museum attendants whose helpfulness is seen to extend beyond the limits of duty. The question of whether or not gratuities should be offered at all is, of course, a controversial one, and teachers must act according to their consciences. It is only realistic, however, to recognize that we do live in a society in which certain practices are recognized and this is one of them. Besides, the offering of a gratuity that has been justifiably earned can create goodwill and go far towards smoothing the way on future visits. Finally, having worked out all the elements of cost it is always a good idea to add a little extra for something which, perhaps, could not be anticipated, but might require expenditure. Any surplus collected in consequence of this can always be returned at the end of the outing.

Collection of monies from pupils

Depending on the nature and type of school as well as on the form of the outing, so will the pupils be charged for the cost, in whole or in part or not at all. On the assumption that a charge will be made, and that either for the total amount or for a proportion, teachers are well advised to begin the collection of this money from pupils as far in advance of the outing as possible. In this respect, a number of simple principles may with profit be borne in mind. In the first place, when teachers collect money from children, receipts should always be given. Secondly it should always be made clear to the participants just exactly what it is that they are being asked to pay for. The corollary is that it should also be made clear to them the exact nature of what is being received either free of charge or at a concession rate. Pupils should, in addition, be advised to convey this information to parents, some of whom may be less reluctant to subscribe when they realize that the outing would have cost a great deal more had it been undertaken privately, and that the children are only being asked for a token payment. In many circumstances, of course, the school would be paying for the entire cost. Apart from the question of economic necessity, there are often sound reasons for encouraging this, especially if the teacher is concerned to promote the notion that the outing is not simply a 'treat' but a rather exciting extension of the work of the classroom.

Preliminary briefing of children

The purpose of this will be principally administrative, as instructions will be given on such matters as time and place of departure and estimated time of return, but, this is also the meeting at which children will be reminded of the educational purpose of the outing. The notion of extending the work of the classroom beyond the confines of the school cannot be too strongly stressed, because it implies that behaviour and attitudes considered appropriate in school are also expected in the new situation where the work of the classroom is held to be continuing. It follows from this that there should be no playing of noisy transistors, nor any kind of horseplay or rowdyism. The fact that some children may have had previous experiences of bus journeys in which one or other of those things happened makes it all the more imperative to stress the teacher's expectations with regard to the out-of-school behaviour of pupils engaged in what should be a well-organized and orderly educational programme. It will help considerably if the teacher can plan in such a way that the pupils have things to do and to look out for on the journey, although the idea of having special worksheets at this stage is not recommended. Whatever the educational advantages may be (and in this context they are debatable), a lurching bus, with all the attendant difficulties that follow from an inability to write properly, or retrieve dropped pencils, is no place for such an exercise. Moreover, where children's attention is alternating between the passing countryside and worksheet, there is an increased probability that someone will be sick. A running commentary by the teacher is much preferred, or a simple reference map or guide to which pupils can occasionally refer. A page reproduced here from a London Transport guide for visitors taking the sightseeing bus trip of central London shows a good style. As the journey progresses the visitor can look to right or left according to the instruction of the guide. Places of interest on the way can be identified from the drawings, and the notes are brief and informative. Something like this would be very useful for an excursion of the kind which we have been considering.

Expectations with regard to pupil behaviour in the museum or on the site itself should be made clear at this time. It goes without saying that the group should be supervised throughout, for that is the task of the teacher and one cannot expect attendants to be child disciplinarians. At the same time, it should be accepted that pupils will require to move about in a museum and will make a certain amount of noise. It is all the more necessary for the teacher to define in advance what is acceptable in this respect and what is not. Evidence of firm (not to be identified with either excessive or oppressive) control will also do much to secure the goodwill of the museum staff.

The briefing meeting is also the time when children should be told about catering arrangements and warned not to bring with them excessive amounts of food and lemonade. If necessary, it should be forbidden, again on the grounds of what are the acceptable behavioural norms of the classroom. The more the teacher can convey the notion that the coach will be an extension of the classroom, the greater the likelihood that pupils will act sensibly

CLEOPATRA'S NEEDLE
(*to your left*). From her city of Heliopolis and over 3,500 years old. Its twin is in Central Park, New York.

SOUTH BANK ARTS CENTRE
(*left—across the river*) consists of the Royal Festival Hall, Queen Elizabeth Hall, Purcell Rooms and the Hayward Gallery.

WESTMINSTER BRIDGE
(*to your left*)

HOUSES OF PARLIAMENT
(*to your left*). The clock tower, 320 feet high, houses 'Big Ben'.

PARLIAMENT SQUARE
(*to your right*) has an assortment of Prime Ministers, Abraham Lincoln and Epstein's controversial Field Marshal Smuts.

WESTMINSTER ABBEY
(*to your left*) founded by Edward the Confessor in 1065. The Abbey has seen every coronation since its foundation.

WHITEHALL
The street of Government. Amid the traffic is the Cenotaph, the memorial to the nation's war dead.

DOWNING STREET
(*to your left*) with No. 10, the official residence of the Prime Minister.

THE BANQUETING HOUSE
(*to your right*) by Inigo Jones (1622). The only remaining building of the ancient Palace of Whitehall.

THE HORSE GUARDS
(*to your left*) by William Kent (about 1750). In front, the splendidly accoutred sentries of the Household Cavalry.

Page from London Transport tour guide

and behave in a responsible way on the day of the outing itself.

It should be made clear to the children the procedure to be followed in the event of one of them becoming lost; this is especially important if some free time is allowed. Indications should be given as to which places are out of bounds, e.g. boating ponds, chair lifts, amusement arcades, cliff edges, etc. It is always advisable, too, to have a few words regarding respect for property. Antisocial behaviour of the kind that leads to destructive acts may well result in a ban, imposed either by the museum or the civic authority, on similar visits in the future by other classes in the school.

Finally, bearing in mind the time of the year and the proposed venue, advice about the clothing to be worn should also be given, i.e. warm or light, protective or otherwise. It is astonishing how some children can turn up ill-prepared for an outing which, one would have thought, logically demanded that certain things be taken.

Progress schedules

In the preparation and organization of any school outing there is inevitably some paper work involved: letters have to be written, replies noted and filed, parental permission forms issued and collected, prepared receipts kept ready for signing and handing out to children. Because of this, a box or wallet file and a packet of elastic bands are necessities, so that the various little bundles of receipts, slips, letters, etc., can be kept together in one place. It is also useful for the teacher in charge of the organizing to keep a planning schedule, so that anyone concerned can tell at a glance how the arrangements are coming along. This makes sense for a number of reasons, not the least of which is that a busy teacher has more to do than try to retain such administrative minutiae in his head. The planning schedule helps to give relief from such a burden. It means, too, that if the organizer should leave, or for some reason be unable to carry on with the preparatory work, then someone else can easily take over, with the partially completed planning schedule available as an indication of what has yet to be done. This means that the planning schedule is in the nature of a classroom record of work; it serves as a reminder of what has been achieved as well as what remains to be undertaken. There need be no set format and, indeed, the best planning schedules are probably those that are tailored by trial and error to fit the requirements of a particular school. Nevertheless, it is still possible to frame a schedule which should have a degree of general applicability. An attempt to do this is embodied in the forms shown here, based largely on the issues mentioned above. Note that they are drawn up with provision for up to three visitation points on the one outing.

HISTORY DEPARTMENT
Planning schedule   Single or half-day outings

Excursion to _ _ _ _ _ _ _ _ _ _ _ _ _ _ _ _ _ _	Class_ _ _ _ _ _ _ _ _ _ _ _ _
Teacher-in-charge _ _ _ _ _ _ _ _ _ _ _ _ _ _	Date of outing _ _ _ _ _ _ _
Headmaster's permission _ _ _ _ _ _ _ _ _	

1. Nature of authority in charge of museum or site

Ref. letter	Name of museum/site	Write to
(a)		
(b)		
(c)		

2. Information to curator or custodian

Ref.	Time	Form of visit	Number of students	Number of staff	Letter sent	Reply	Permission
(a)							
(b)							
(c)							

3. Any special conditions required

(a) _

(b) _

(c) _

4. Admission charges

(a) _____ (b)_____ (c) _____

5. Concession entry

Ref.	Name of museum/site	Sanctioned	Refused	Supervision ratio
(a)				
(b)				
(c)				

6. Facilities available

Ref.	Personal guides	Study guides	Intra-mural lectures	Work direc-tives	Clip boards	Pencils	Stools
(a)							
(b)							
(c)							

7. Route information

Parking _____
_____

Public conveniences _____
_____

Possible hazards _____
_____

8. Sketch maps

9. Coach transport

Hirer _   Phone No._ _ _ _ _ _ _ _ _ _ _

Size of coach required _ _ _ _ _ _ _ _ _ _ _   Cost_ _ _ _ _ _ _ _ _ _ _ _ _ _

Booking made on _ _ _ _ _ _ _ Confirmation received on _ _ _ _ _ _ _ _

Account discharged on_ _ _ _ _ _ _ _ _ _   Receipt No._ _ _ _ _ _ _ _ _ _

10. Rail transport

British Rail _ _ _ _ _ _ _ _ _ _ _ _ _ _ _ _ _ _   Phone No._ _ _ _ _ _ _ _ _ _ _

Compartment/seat reservations _ _ _ _ _ _ _ _ Total cost _ _ _ _ _ _ _ _ _

Booking made on_ _ _ _ _ _ _ _ Confirmation received on _ _ _ _ _ _ _

Account discharged on _ _ _ _ _ _ _ _ _ _ _   Receipt No._ _ _ _ _ _ _ _ _ _

Movement to and from station_ _

11. Staff responsibilities   * = Staff member in overall charge

Catering _

Litter box _

First-aid box _

Clip boards, directives, pencils_ _

Counting heads_ _

Site supervision _

Additional_ _

_ _

12. Insurance cover

Company_ _ _ _ _ _ _ _ _ _ _ _ _ _ _ _ _ _ _   Phone No._ _ _ _ _ _ _ _ _ _ _

Duration of cover _ _ _ _ _ _ _ _ _ _ _ _ _ _   Premium _ _ _ _ _ _ _ _ _ _ _ _

Special conditions_ _

Premium paid_ _ _ _ _ _ _ _ _ _ _ _ _ _ _ _ _   Policy No.'_ _ _ _ _ _ _ _ _ _ _

13. Parental permission

Number of pupils _ _ _ _ _ _ _ _ Number of slips received_ _ _ _ _ _ _ _

Slips not returned (names) _

_ _

_ _

14. Journey schedule

Place	Leave for	Arrive at	Place	Leave for	Arrive at

15. Total estimated expense

Transport _____

_____

_____

Entry fees _____

_____

_____

Gratuities _____

Extras _____   Total _____

16. Money collected from pupils

Date_____ Amount _____ | Balance b/f _____

Date_____ Amount _____ | Date_____ Amount _____

Date_____ Amount _____ | Date_____ Amount _____

Date_____ Amount _____ | Date_____ Amount _____

Balance c/f _____ | Total _____

Money outstanding from:

_____

_____

_____

17. Briefing

Date_____ Time _____ Place_____

Points to be covered _____

_____

_____

_____

_____

18. Brief report on visit

_____

_____

_____

_____

_____

_____

_____

4

Work Directives

When are they appropriate?
Before considering the factors involved in the construction of work
directives for use within a museum or on a visit to a historical site,
one needs to examine the reasons for having them at all. There are
certainly many teachers, just as there are museum and site curators,
who have reservations about their use, some rejecting them altogether and others accepting their validity only in certain recognized
circumstances. It would probably be true to say that there can be no
hard-and-fast rule about a matter of this kind. Like many other
educational issues, it is not soluble in terms of a single formula, but
depends upon a number of features, not the least of which would be
the stage of development reached by the pupils and the character of
the place which it is intended to visit.

Consider, for example, a situation in which, as part of an overseas
school excursion, a group of children are taken to visit the remains
of the ancient roman city of Pompeii. Whatever the theory may be,
and whatever one may have done on any previous organized visits,
this is emphatically not an occasion for standing at the entrance in
order to hand out work directives to the children as they enter the
area of the excavations. One's first visit to a place like Pompeii ought
rightly to be preceded by a certain amount of preparatory study, so
that it may be appreciated to the full, but when the special and
long-anticipated moment arrives the initial impact upon the senses
should not be blunted by the competing preoccupation of a work
directive. In a sense, it is a matter of timing. On a subsequent
occasion, if the opportunity presented itself, it might be appropriate
to attempt something with the same group, but it would be both
misguided and insensitive to assume that on a first visit to such a

place it could be either desirable or appropriate. In certain respects this is simply another way of expressing the notion that educational aims require to be clear and seen to be related to pupils' needs. Much recent debate has centred on the need to define objectives and in history, as in other disciplines, this has led to an increasing concern for identifying cognitive skills and relating them to the teaching of history in schools. Cognition, however, is not all, for attention has also to be paid to the part which historical study has to play in the development of emotional response. This is what has been termed the 'affective' as distinct from the 'cognitive' element and many educational theorists are worried at the difficulty not simply of measuring the affective element, but of identifying and defining it. This particular philosophical *impasse* need not concern us. For practical purposes what matters is that the teacher should endeavour to develop an intuitive feeling for the situation, so that inappropriate procedures are shunned and every opportunity seized to develop the visit in the best way possible. It is worth remembering that long before modern educational psychology invented and distinguished between such esoterically labelled areas of human action as 'cognitive' and 'affective', A. N. Whitehead had already pointed towards the desirability of first encouraging the 'romance' stage of learning, as a necessary precondition of the kind of systematized investigation which would nowadays be subsumed under the label 'cognitive'. What it amounts to, in simple terms, is ensuring that when preparatory study has pointed the way to a climax point, the enriching experience once arrived at, whether it be a visit to the Louvre or a tramcar ride at Crich, should be savoured and enjoyed as an end in itself.

The relevance of the study guide

Are we then to reject all forms of support and direction? One feels that this would be wholly unjustified, for what is in dispute is not the validity and appropriateness of support but rather the imposition on the pupil of the kind of tasks which, while highly relevant to most museum or site visits, have much less to commend them in the situation just considered. For those rather special occasions which we have been discussing, and in particular those first-time visits, something in the nature of a study guide can be recommended. This

59

type of aid is of particular value for an introductory visit, because there is no built-in pattern of tasks directing the children to work on specific themes in the galleries or on the site. In certain circumstances it could take the form of a simple commentary, with inserted directions to look at certain exhibits along the way. It could be presented either on paper as a study guide, or in some kind of electronically recorded form, for example on a tape-cassette. Of the two, the printed study guide is probably the easier to produce for a sizeable group. On the other hand the advantage of the tape-recorded presentation lies in the ease with which the young visitor can keep his eyes on the exhibits throughout the guided commentary. Whichever form is adopted will obviously depend on convenience and the resources available. Both are essentially modes of providing a means of self-direction, in order to enable the visitor to embark with confidence on an unescorted tour of the relevant exhibits, but without being required, in the process of doing this, to undertake any practical or written activity of the kind normally associated with the worksheet directive. An extract from a Sound-guide tour of Fountain's Hall has already been given. Here is a similar example, this time set out in print form as part of a duplicated study guide for the use of children visiting Bolling Hall, Bradford.

> This particular kitchen would also be devoted to dairy work, making butter and cheese. If you turn right now, with the press at your back, look to the right hand corner, you will see two old upright churns, and you made butter in them by working the wooden plunger through the lid, up and down, up and down, it really was back-breaking work.

> Now a quick look up at the roof, that wooden frame is not for drying clothes, it is called a haver, where the baked oat cakes as they are called in the West Riding were hung for storage.

Like the example of Fountain's Hall, the material in the study guide could be presented in tape-cassette form. There are, however, some guides which could not be so easily translated, and especially when some element of illustrative material is incorporated. The accompanying example of the visitors' guide to the Washington estate at Mount Vernon, Virginia, demonstrates this. In it the notes on the historical material are accompanied not by interspersed route directions but by a site map. From the point of view of designing a study guide, the example is of interest for another reason, in that it

A PERSPECTIVE VIEW
—— of the ——
Mansion, Out-buildings, Gardens, etc.,
with a key thereto

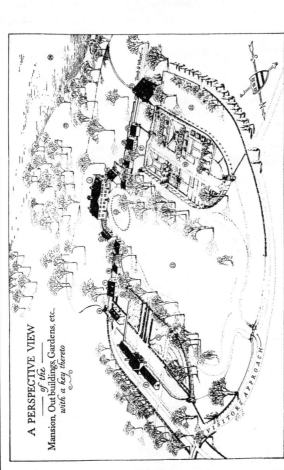

1) *Mansion*—In anticipation of George Washington's marriage in 1759 the structure was repaired and enlarged from one and one-half to two and one-half stories. Shortly before the Revolution, Washington made plans for additions at each end of the house. These additions were not completed until 1787.

2) *Greenhouse and Quarters*—Original structures were destroyed by fire in 1835. They have been reconstructed on the basis of documentary and archeological evidence.

3) *Flower Garden*—An eighteenth-century garden. The boxwood hedges are believed to have been planted to 17— to edge the flower beds in which are displayed flowering plants similar to eighteenth century Virginians.

4) *Icehouse.*

5) *Museum*—Erected in 1928 to provide suitable display space for memorabilia.

6) *Botanical Garden*—Used by General Washington for experimental planting. The area has been re-cleared and replanted.

7) *Spinning House and Quarters*—Twelve or more people were regularly employed in the textile crafts at Mount Vernon.

8) *Storehouse*—Used for storage of salt and miscellaneous farm equipment.

9) *Gardener's House*—The records indicate that this building was used from time to time by the gardener, the shoemaker and the tailor. A part of the building may also have been used to accommodate the sick.

10) *Office*—The domestic records indicate a sequence of uses for this building: servants hall, guest house, manager's residence and office. It is now an administrative office.

12) *Courtyard*—Posts and chains have been restored. The dial post supports the original sundial.

13) *Bowling Green*—Developed by General Washington in 178?. A few of the larger trees bordering the driveway are believed to have been planted at that time.

14) *Kitchen*—Equipped with utensils of the period, some original.

15) *Storehouse and Overseers' Quarters*—A storekeeper distributed tools and equipment from the front room. A number of the staff was domiciled in the small rooms behind the storeroom.

16) *Smokehouse.*

17) *Laundry Yard.*

18) *Washhouse*—This building has been furnished with appropriate equipment of the period, in accordance with the evidence contained in the inventories made by General Washington's executors.

19) *Coachhouse*—Rebuilt on the original site in 1894.

20) *Kitchen Garden*—Restored within the original enclosing walls in a manner true to the time of General Washington.

21) *Stable*—Built in 1782 to replace a frame stable which was destroyed by fire the previous year.

22) *Paddock.*

23) *Park.*

24) *Potomac River.*

Public rest rooms are located beneath the Museum—⊞ on plan at left.

Handbooks, and other official publications may be purchased in the sixteen-sided west end of ⊞ on the plan.

Visitors' guide to the Mount Vernon Estate, Virginia

effectively demonstrates that a good guide should never be so over-elaborate as to dominate the attention of the user. The aim should be to design something that will do the job, yet require such minimal consultation as to leave the visitor free to focus the major part of his attention on what the museum or site has to offer. For a historical site in particular, this approach is to be specially recommended as admirably suitable for visiting school groups, for it has the triple advantages of simplicity, attractiveness and adequacy. Such a single sheet guide is particularly commendable for visits to museums or sites where the study areas are spread out. Further, if the venue is one where the children might wish to take photographs then a guide of this kind lends itself readily to the inclusion of simple suggestion as to the best vantage points. Information like this could be indicated by a simple asterisk system.

The purpose of the work directive

Notwithstanding all that has been said in advocacy of the use of study guides, any serious use of a museum or historical site, especially over a period, is likely to mean the adoption of more extended material, and it is appropriate to turn now to a consideration of what has already been referred to as the work directive or worksheet. This differs from the study guide, principally as being more demanding in terms of pupil activity and involvement. In practical terms, this usually means that pupils are expected not only to look and observe, but to record the results of those observations—descriptive, analytical and deductive—in writing. There need be no essential contradiction with procedures already advocated, and involving either a free browse or, at the most, the use of a non-intrusive study guide. Now we are thinking in terms of directing pupils' attention more specifically towards certain things and asking for their views and opinions on what they see. There comes a time when they are ready for something of this nature, and it is wrong to see it as some kind of restrictive mechanism that circumscribes initiative and somehow detracts from the value of the visit as a free and imaginative experience. Properly conceived, there is every reason for believing that the well-planned and attractive work directive can stimulate interest and direct attention to what might otherwise be missed.

Thus far the argument has centred on positive aspects of work directives concerned with motivation, the sustaining of interest and the direction of effort towards particular goals. There is another side to this which is only too familiar to many museum curators. It is the ease with which undirected visits, to museums in particular, can only too often degenerate with alarming rapidity into either a kind of wild undisciplined disorder, the ethos of which is 'anything for a lark', or else be productive of an atmosphere of indifferent apathy, characterized by a communal boredom that infects the whole party. Admittedly this is to view the undirected museum visit at its least productive level, but to many of those responsible for custodianship it is certain to be a recognizable situation. To put it in another way, it must not be naïvely assumed that if one lets children loose in a museum then, by some mystical aesthetic and intellectual trans-mogrification they will somehow achieve the enriching and imaginative experience that one would wish them to have. One cannot, of course, generalize from such a pessimistic standpoint. There are those occasions, particularly of first-glimpse wonder, when both individuals and groups are inspired without any stimulus beyond what they have gone to see. However that may be, this historical empathy cannot always be guaranteed, so that in all such circumstances there is always the risk that the museum visit may turn out to be at best a flop, at worst a disaster, simply for lack of the little direction which could have served to stimulate the young visitors and kept their interest channelled along profitable lines.

Of course, to talk about the inspirational value of work directives is to make certain assumptions about them, not the least of which is that they should have the character to inspire. The fact that this is not always so makes them, from an educational point of view, double-edged weapons, capable of making a difficult situation worse. Where the content is suspect, or ineffectively related to the exhibits, or there is a significant variation in the level of clarity from item to item, or a lack of consistency in the amount of space left for answers—more than adequate in some cases and much less so in others—or an untidiness in presentation due either to typing errors or indistinct printing, there is likely to be diminished motivation on the part of the users, such factors acting as disincentives to any extension of interest in enquiry and research.

Compilation of directives

How then are we to go about the task of drafting work directives which will satisfy the best professional standards? As a preliminary, the compiler should assess the detailed nature of the museum or site: for example, if it is a museum collection, to note how it is housed, to what pattern the exhibits are arranged and the form which the labelling takes. The particular character of the museum may influence the style of questioning in the worksheet. The specialist museum often offers an opportunity for finding groups of exhibits in typological sequence, and the compiler should be on the look out for comparable and contrasting items which demonstrate change and development. On the other hand, the folk museum, which is more concerned with reflecting the life of the community over a period, is likely to be productive of a different style of questioning, perhaps concerned with highlighting the history of local crafts. This preliminary stage is also the time for assessing the museum's potential, with particular reference to the line of specialist study that the pupils will be pursuing. The teacher must be on guard, and resist the temptation to be sidetracked, either towards something that is not relevant or to exhibits which, though superficially more attractive, are of less practical value for the immediate purpose. The teacher who goes to inspect the antiquities of Roman Britain in the British Museum may find the Mildenhall Treasure of absorbing interest, but if the purpose of the visit is to investigate the Museum's potential in respect of armour and weapons, that is what he must concentrate on.

Once the preliminaries are over the task of designing the work directive can be undertaken. In carrying this out, there are a number of basic principles to be observed and these can now be considered in turn. In the first place, questions should not be obscure or ambiguous. Many of us, at some time or another, have had the experience of purchasing something mechanical or electrical for the home, only to experience considerable difficulty in making sense of inadequate accompanying instructions. On reflection, most people would probably agree that the principal reaction to this type of situation is one of frustration. Similarly, this is the emotion which pupils are likely to manifest when they are unable to comprehend exactly what is wanted in a work directive. This applies particularly if the teacher is not immediately available to help solve the problem of initial interpretation. Even with the teacher on hand as a source of reference, it is still undesirable that he or she should progress, in the manner of the Pied Piper of Hamelin, through the museum or around the site, with a permanent tail of young enquirers, as will surely happen if the directive contains items that are imprecise, or ambiguously worded in terms of the set tasks. Clarity, therefore, should be regarded as a prime requisite of good compilation.

A second desirable feature is the inclusion of a range of items that display variation in style and level throughout the directive. This implies planning in such a way that pupils are invited not only to observe and record, but also to undertake analysis and deduction, involving comparison and contrast. In practical terms, this means that the designing of a work directive that is to be educationally valuable is an exercise that requires thought. A directive which concentrated solely upon the assembly of easily ascertainable factual knowledge would be likely to make minimal demands on both the learner and the person responsible for its collation. To say this is not to assert that questions inviting simple observation and recording should be entirely absent. On the contrary, quite apart from the value of items like, 'What is the name on the fire engine?', as useful introductory leads to other lines of investigation, their inclusion as ends in themselves is warranted since part of the historian's job is to acquire facts. In certain circumstances, there is even a case for asking questions that invite a simple 'Yes' or 'No', if only to serve as a means of keeping the student on the correct track. But it would be difficult to justify a work directive which never rose above the level of seeking only basic facts or that merely demanded straight positive or negative responses. It could be argued, of course, that such simple directives might be well suited to the needs of the less able. The view is worthy of respect, because pupils of comparatively low academic ability are likely to make more of questions which lean towards observation rather than deductive analysis. Nevertheless, here too an effort should be made to include more demanding elements, in order to maximize the educational gain for the participants. The fact that a work directive designed for the use of the less able pupil might be weighted strongly in favour of the simpler type of factual question need never preclude attempts to put in items that make greater demands, provided their inclusion is not inconsistent with the primary principle of matching the tasks to the age, ability and aptitude of the learners.

With this in mind, what is the justification for going beyond recorded observation and inviting additional comment on reasons for similarities or differences, or causal connections or consequences? The answer is simple. What such intellectual exercises have in common is that they are all ways in which a pupil's thoughts may be turned towards that most historical of mental pursuits, rational observation and the formation of conclusions from the evidence. Just how easy such 'higher order' items are to compile depends upon a number of factors, not least of which is that one has to work within the limits of what is available in the museum or on the site. There is no doubt that they present a challenge to the compiler beyond what is required of simpler question forms, yet they need be neither elaborate nor involved. This point can best be illustrated with a simple example.

The Glasgow Museum of Transport has a single-deck tramcar, dating from 1898. Designed to the style of the American street car, it was built with a central entrance leading to a saloon on either side. One of these sections was well upholstered, had glass in the windows and was reserved for non-smokers; the other had wooden seats, open sides, and smoking was permitted. In directing attention in the museum to those features, one might simply ask, 'Are there differences between the front and rear portions of the tram?' The question is designed to elicit a simple positive or negative response, but its style need not be seen as detracting from its value as a pointer. Indeed, the affirmation or negation is virtually superfluous, and the item might just as easily have been presented in the form of a statement such as one might expect to find in a study guide. For example, 'Look at the front and rear portions of the tram and notice the differences between them.' The same subject could have been used for observation and recording by asking, 'What are the main differences which you can spot between the front and rear portions of the tram?' In this case the pupil would be expected to list his conclusions in the appropriate space provided in the work directive.

In each of these three examples, the material is treated in a straightforward way, and they all have it in common that the youngster is asked not only to observe, but to compare and contrast as well. The last example given, however, could have been put in a different manner by asking, 'What differences in seating and ventilation were there between the "smoking" and "non-smoking" sections of the tram?' In this there would have been the hint of a causal connection between the 'smoking' factor and the fact that the tram was built and furnished in such a way as to ensure that seat upholstery was not burnt, nor the air unnecessarily polluted. By changing the question wording a little more, it is possible to direct attention explicitly to this possibility. Alternatives, in progressive order of difficulty, might be,

- 'Why do you think that the "smoking" section of the tram had no upholstery on the seats, and no glass in the windows?'
- 'Does the fact that there were "smoking" and "non-smoking" sections help to explain differences in the design of the front and rear portions of the tram?'
- 'Is there anything that you can see that suggests a reason why the front and rear portions of the tram were built and furnished in different styles?'

Getting beyond the simpler type of question often requires a determined effort, but the gain is immeasurably worth while. One has to bear in mind, however, that work directives can legitimately display a varying level of difficulty and, indeed, it is probably desirable that they should do so.

To conclude on this point, and for the particular benefit of those who may be about to embark for the first time on a compilation exercise of this kind, it may be of interest to note that when inspiration lies dormant, a visit to the sales stall is to be recommended. Most museums and sites have inexpensive guide material for sale, and a quick read through the appropriate section often triggers off ideas.

A third important principle to be determined is the extent to which one is justified in assuming that pupils are likely to be in possession of knowledge that is not readily available within the museum or site itself. Now, as a rule, a work directive should generally be a fairly self-contained affair, so that normally the visitor can undertake and complete it largely on the basis of what he sees. This is not to deny the desirability, emphasized elsewhere in this book, of interrelating information and impressions gleaned from other sources, but simply to assert that, unless the teacher has planned otherwise, then during the actual performance of the task, the pupils should be able to gather most of their information and draw whatever conclusions are necessary from an examination of what is on display. In cases where dependence on outside information is required, it is the teacher's duty to see to it that pupils are either sufficiently prepared in advance of the visit, or else are offered access to this information during its course. The teacher, for example, might make certain necessary book sources available for pupil reference. Only in situations where the outside information is of such a nature that one could reasonably assume it to be already within the general knowledge of the pupils is there justification in dispensing with such help. An example of this, which is used in the next chapter, is that one could, with confidence, expect pupils to know that a church bride's dress is normally white. This would be a reasonable assumption. On the other hand, to assume that the same pupils could match this with an equal knowledge of the name of the Foreign Secretary would be unreasonable. This is information which one has no right to expect them to possess unless they have previously been directed to it, by formal teaching or otherwise. In compiling work directives, one way round this difficulty is to provide a short piece of information as a preamble to the question itself.

Recording of answers

So much for the drafting of the items destined to make up the work content of the proposed directive. The compiler must then consider its format. In essence, of course, the museum work directive is not significantly different from any other, however designated (e.g. work card, worksheet, assignment card, etc.) which the pupil is likely to encounter within the classroom. The increasing tendency in schools to fragment the teaching—learning experience into work group or independent study situations has led to a growing dependence on the use of study directives of various kinds. Unlike the classroom directive, however, which is not expendable but is intended for the ongoing use of pupils in some kind of rotation, the work directive designed for the museum or site has a limited life. The reason for this is basically a matter of convenience. Within the classroom a directive can be used by a succession of pupils on any number of occasions because there are adequate opportunities for them to record their findings elsewhere. This can take the form of writing up a work book, making a frieze, constructing a model, or any other appropriate activity. The directive itself is not used for recording. By contrast, on the outside visit the administrative emphasis has to be on what is both feasible and practical, so that the need is for self-containment, with a style of work material that caters for recording as well as direction. One cannot expect children to handle unwieldy work books on top of everything else which they may be required to take with them on the visit. It follows that the designs of directives intended for use in museums or sites should make provision for the insertion of children's answers and observations. Nor is it sufficient simply to pay lip-service to this need: to reiterate a point already made, nothing is more frustrating to the user than to find that the spaces allocated for the recording of answers are inadequate, either in respect of size or numbers.

Appearance of directives

The desirability of presenting attractively designed work directives has also to be borne in mind. In particular, false economies need to be avoided. Whatever the simple economic advantages may be in terms of both cost and preparation time, directives should not be in tightly packed lines of typescript. Moreover, if the typing style is amateurish then, however well intentioned, its overall effect may be unfortunate. A directive which in style and layout is pleasing to the eye is much more likely to be an incentive to effort than one which gives the impression of careless or slovenly construction.

In matters of presentation individual teachers are likely to have their own notions as to what is desirable and this will be in part determined by a consideration of the stage and ability of those pupils who are to use the material. Nevertheless, whatever the particular inclinations of a teacher may be, the following suggestions are offered as simple guide lines to the designing of work directives, the object of which is to arouse and sustain pupil interest for reasons other than their intrinsic contents.

1. A full margin should be left all round the four sides of the sheet, so that the material does not appear crowded. An additional

advantage is that it allows a pupil scope for making marginal notes on any item which particularly interests him.

2. Items should be arranged neatly on the sheet, with sections correctly headed, consistency in the type face used and adequate spacing between lines. Items should also be positioned with care and in a regular relationship one to another.

3. All items should be numbered or lettered, as much for neatness of presentation as for ease of reference.

4. Wherever possible some illustrative material should be included. More than anything else, this enhances the attraction of the work-sheet. Some care ought also to be given to its positioning on the page. Where, for example, a page has to carry two or three separate illustrations, it might be better to set them off alternately on the left and right rather than place them down one side in columnar fashion.

5. Where more than one sheet is compiled, an occasional change in style is recommended. By altering the form of presentation of both printed and illustrative material, in however small a way, variety is introduced and the interest of using the directive is enhanced. There may be limitations on the extent to which this can be done, perhaps because of the nature of the museum or site itself. Yet, even if the alterations are minor ones, it is still good policy to introduce them in order to avoid a standard format.

Illustrative material

This is probably a good point at which to consider in more detail the various aspects of illustrative material in work directives and, in particular, the different ways in which it can be used.

Generally speaking, illustration can be either decorative or functional, or both. The purely decorative might be found in a directive where, almost as an afterthought, some appropriate border or heading is included for no other reason than to give it a pleasing style and appearance. In such a case, the purpose is simply adornment, the primary intention being neither to direct nor to stimulate further work, except in so far as it might be reasonable to assume that increased motivation would be more likely to follow on from an attractive rather than from an unattractive directive.

Most illustration is, nevertheless, functional rather than decorative, and this may take various forms. In the first place, the direction of attention towards a particular object can often be encouraged by the inclusion of a simple sketch, especially in cases where some doubt might arise as to what was being indicated. Visual clarification of this kind has an identifying function and should be accompanied by questions on the exhibit itself.

Presentation of ready-made illustration is one thing, but work produced by pupils is a different matter, not so much concerned with initial identification as with a graphic form of recording what has been found out during the examination of the exhibit. The value of sometimes leaving a suitable blank space on a work directive in order that a pupil may attempt the freehand drawing of an item need not be in dispute. In cases where the task is relatively easy, this is a perfectly valid practice. What is less defensible is the view that it should be normal procedure, and that free expression should never be restricted. There are two valid arguments against this. The first is that children's skill in the graphic arts extends over a wide spectrum, so that a percentage of pupils may experience difficulty in undertaking drawing other than that which is simple and straightforward. The fact that this percentage is likely to increase according to the complexity of the task makes it necessary to consider whether one is justified in introducing such a level of difficulty as part of an ancillary and rather minor accompaniment to a visit. In any cross-section of an average school population, there will be children whose ability to see spatial relationships is so poor that they are likely to produce drawings of ridiculously minute size, which tell nothing of the object under examination, or in which the parts are disproportionately arranged to produce something quite grotesque. In such circumstances there is every likelihood that a number of the participants themselves may well feel unhappy about their drawings, and this may be a disincentive to further effort. In this respect it is worth remembering that an inability to sketch effectively does not imply any suspension of self-critical judgment, and it is this which could so readily act as an inhibiting influence, reducing motivation towards subsequent museum work.

A second qualifying factor is the need to be clear about objectives and to recognize that the nature of the exercise is primarily historical appreciation. The implication of this, with the basic assumption that part of the historian's task is accurate recording, is that certain limitations must be accepted in respect of free artistic expression undertaken in any such context.

For these two reasons, it is sometimes more in keeping with the spirit of the enquiry to offer initial assistance by presenting on the work directive a part of the required illustration. For example, two adjacent circles of appropriate size might be given, with the accompanying invitation to 'Draw the penny-farthing bicycle'. In this way, children with poor graphic skill would be given a helpful start, while for most there would be a reasonable guarantee that the essential historical nature of the object was effectively recorded. The applicability of this will be readily appreciated by those who have seen children in the frustrating situation of being unable even to start on the task.

Any part of the illustration may be offered already prepared, but the most satisfactory is usually a general outline, as in the examples shown here.

Lady with parasol, 1855

Steam fire engine, 1863

The decision about which style to adopt will depend very much on the shape of the exhibit in question. It is important, however, to keep the guide lines clear, so that the referents are identifiable. To produce a hotch-potch in which disconnected bits and pieces of the object are laid out in no recognizable shape or relationship, is merely to be obtuse, without making any effective attack on the original problem.

Once the details have been sketched, the illustration can either be left, or else shaded or coloured in (within the museum or site or back at school, whichever is the more convenient). Where appropriate, the parts may be labelled for subsequent consultation, and it is interesting to note that this approach has been developed in a most effective and imaginative way by the National Army Museum for the study of army uniform and weaponry. The child is supplied with two sheets of paper (reproduced below). One is a standard printed sheet, with a blank figure in the centre, a left-hand column for labels and a space on the right for drawing a weapon. The other sheet is gummed on the back, and may be one of a selection of three

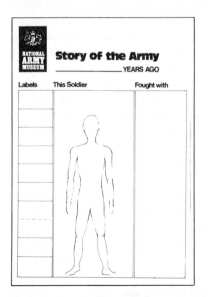
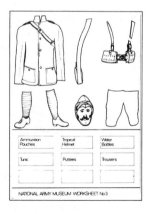

Directive material from National Army Museum

which deal respectively with soldiers' uniforms of 1700, 1800 and 1900. Each gummed sheet has outline drawings of the bits and pieces of the uniform concerned, as well as the appropriate identifying labels. No date is given, nor is there any indication as to the colour of the uniform. This means that the child has, first, to find the original in the Story of the Army Gallery. Having done this, he fills in the date at the top of his first sheet, cuts out the uniform pieces from the gummed sheet, fits them to the figure outline and colours in the completed drawing. The museum supplies scissors and coloured pencils. On the right of the printed sheet, he is expected to draw a weapon (preferably a musket or rifle) of the same period. It only remains to stick on the labels and run neat lines from them to the corresponding parts on the completed figure. To accomplish this last part of the total activity, children may have to do some checking in the Uniform Gallery, which is in another part of the Museum. Guidance as to which exhibit cases are the relevant ones is given to the teacher, so that if children get into difficulties, these can be remedied fairly quickly.

Something very similar is produced by the Museum of Costume in Bath. A series of cards with cut-out figures and costume are available for a number of nineteenth-century fashions. The style of presentation would suggest that the compilers had in mind the idea that they might be cut out and made up back at school. Nevertheless, there are obvious advantages if the pupil can at least colour in the outlines during the visit itself, in circumstances where it is still possible to consult the cased exhibits for guidance. This is the kind of thing which is guaranteed to appeal to pupils over a wide age range. The examples quoted from both of those museums represent well thought out and interesting types of work directive and it will be appreciated that the method could be applied to a range of possibilities in areas of historical study other than that of costume.

Before leaving the theme of illustration, one other useful kind of item is worth noting. Strictly speaking, the statistical table is not so much an illustration as a convenient linear framework within which the results of a particular set of observations can be set out. An example of the type of exercise where this is appropriate is one in which the aim is to get the pupil thinking about two or more things and noting briefly specific points of similarity and difference. The

THE
MUSEUM OF COSTUME
CUT-OUT DOLL
1830

THE ASSEMBLY ROOMS, BATH

BEND BACK ALONG THIS LINE

Cut-out material, Museum of Costume, Bath

hope is that in tabulating the features he may be able to observe a pattern of change. If it should manifest itself as a series of improvements, then the pupil may be led to some tangible appreciation of the nature of historical progress. By way of example, here is an item from a work directive for schools made up for a visit to the Victoria and Albert Museum. The invitation is to take a critical look at some of the exhibits in one of the cases in Costume Court:

8. Try to complete the following table, in order to show the principal differences between a gentleman's full-dress coat of 1700 and that of 1780. The first item is already completed in order to indicate what is required.

	1700	1780
Fitting	Loose	Slim
Sleeves		
Cuffs		
Collar		
Cloth used		

Other statistical devices, such as histograms or graphs, can also be used, according to the nature of the subject being studied.

Finally, just as answer space is given for replies to questions, so too should provision be made for any drawing that is required. It is also desirable that pupils' attention be directed to that provision. Simply requesting them to 'Draw the Roman pot', is no certain guarantee that every participant will automatically put it in the appropriate space. An obvious alternative like 'Draw the Roman pot in the space alongside', gets round the problem quite simply.

Tasks on historical sites

All that has been said in the current chapter with regard to the compilation of work directives is, in general, applicable equally to historical sites and museums. In either case, the nature of the investigation is likely to follow broadly similar lines, so that the format of the directive need not differ substantially between one and the other. Certainly there is often less overt information given on the site than in the museum. One commonly finds fewer opportunities for taking advantage of neatly labelled and classified exhibits, carrying not only the name and date of the object but an explanatory note as well. Very often the most that is encountered in the site situation is the identifying notice headed 'Refectory' or 'North Gate' or (that children's delight) 'Dungeons'. This need not prevent the work directive from being designed in much the same way as for a museum visit, to include both text and illustrations, as well as a variety of exploratory items which invite a range of activity from the acquisition of simple factual information to the exercise of those more exacting skills appropriate to the interpretation of evidence.

When one considers the nature of the tasks relevant to a visit to a historical site it is possible to point to certain situations where they might be identical to or markedly different in character from those pertaining to a museum visit. Where there is a collection of preserved material housed indoors within the site precincts, the tasks set need not be dissimilar from those which would be relevant were the same exhibits located elsewhere: it is still essentially a museum situation. It may be that in such circumstances the absence of a multiplicity of exhibits which can be compared and contrasted will restrict the scope of the operation, although this would not be applicable in all instances, for example, in some of the bigger and more important sites, such as the Tower of London or the Palace of Holyroodhouse. On the other hand, whatever the paucity of material, there is no adequate substitute for being on the spot where it all happened.

For outside work, many historical sites are ideally suited for activity-based enquiries quite different in nature from those normally applicable to museums. Simple surveying is a fairly obvious one and is appropriate to any number of outdoor locations. The fundamental exercise is measuring. It is all very well to tell a class that the base of Hadrian's Wall varied in width from 8 to 10 Roman feet and that in some parts it was as narrow as 6. How much better, should the opportunity present itself, to take the children to the remains of the Wall and have them actually work it out for themselves. A surveyor's tape is one of the most useful aids but, failing this, there are two very effective substitutes which are easily improvised. The first is a ten foot length of rope or cord with a knot in it at each one foot point. Extensive measurements can then be taken by counting the number of rope lengths and, for the last little bit, the number of knot intervals. A distance of 34 feet, for example, would be three full lengths of the rope and an additional four knot intervals. The second is an ordinary measuring tape of the kind available from a haberdashery counter. This would allow for finer measuring of the kind appropriate to an examination of windows, doorways, pillar dimensions and so on.

Finding out the height of a building is another interesting exercise, and there are a number of ways in which this may be done, some more sophisticated than others. Since it would be unrealistic to assume a knowledge of trigonometry, an effective, though admittedly less accurate, method is to take a simple sighting on the object concerned, for example a castle tower. This is done by placing a pole in an upright position in the ground and, from a point at ground level exactly one pole's length further back from the point at which it enters the

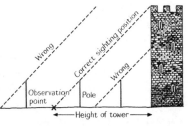

Finding the height of a building

ground, taking a sighting on to the tower through the upper tip of the pole. If the sighting extends to a point somewhere above the top of the tower, then the pole is positioned too far away; if the sighting line strikes the tower at a point lower than its top part, the pole is too near. Once the correct position is attained, the height of the tower can be ascertained by measuring the distance from its base to the point beyond the pole from which the correct sighting was taken.

It will be appreciated that with such a rough and ready method there is considerable scope for error. This can be minimized by attempting the exercise only on a level site, and by ensuring that the sighting is taken from a point as close to the ground as it is possible to get. For all that, investigation of this kind and the recording of results can be a fascinating pursuit, and there is no more effective way of drawing the attention of a group of children to the significant physical features of a building or foundation than by having them gauge and note its dimensions. Simple improvised equipment is all that is necessary, and many a successful field study expedition has been undertaken with little beyond a tape measure, a surveyor's pole (tent or scout poles make effective substitutes) and, for additional interest, a pocket compass. Teachers who try out such uncomplicated methods as are suggested in the example may wish later to graduate to the use of a plane table and an alidade for more advanced work. These are quite easy to use and provide fuller opportunities for this kind of work.

Sketches of various kinds can be undertaken, subject to the qualifications already entered about the likely range of graphic skills in an average school class. A relatively ambitious example is shown opposite, of Richmond Castle in Yorkshire. However, the task can be simplified, not only in the ways already suggested, but also by reducing its scope, for example, by drawing a window, a door or a tower, rather than the whole building.

Another form of pictorial recording on a site is by means of photography. A pupil who possesses a camera could be supplied with a film and commissioned to act as official photographer to the party. What is sketched or photographed will, of course, depend on the character of the investigation and the extent to which interest is focused on the site in general or on specific things, such as the traces

Richmond Castle, Yorkshire

Norman doorway, Bishopstone, Wiltshire

of previous building still to be seen on the brickwork of the existing walls.

Observation of archaeological evidence is a most useful direction for activity to take during a school visit to a historical site. Examining the site in relation to its surroundings, by looking at an Ordnance Survey map, is another. The information and deductions to be drawn from studying the place from complementary facets can then be combined into a rounded picture that tells more of the historical significance of the site than would be the case were attention confined to one element alone, For example, a visit to Durham Cathedral could profitably concentrate on the many Norman features of its massive architecture. This would include the famous choir vaulting, the incised pillars in the nave and the superbly beautiful Galilee chapel. A walk round the outside with a map of reasonable scale can explain much in addition and, in particular, shed light on the reasons for the survival of Durham's holy place, especially from the marauding Scots who never succeeded in taking it. Outside observation with the map reveals that the cathedral is built on a high commanding place which has the natural advantages of being a peninsula, bounded on three sides by the River Wear. The geographical term for

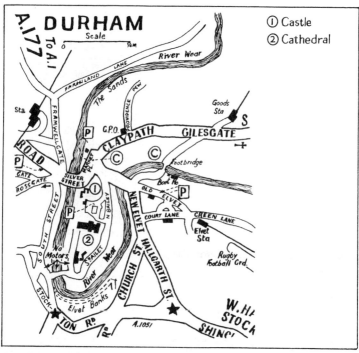

Durham on an 'incised meander'

this is an 'incised meander', and the strategic placing of the ancient Norman castle at the neck of the peninsula virtually guaranteed impregnability for the medieval defenders of Durham.

Imaginative expression can also find scope in a visit to a historical site, for there are fewer places more suitable than the original location for inspiring the young visitor. This is why castle forecourts or abbey ruins are so often chosen for the mounting of historical tableaux. Nor should teachers ignore the opportunity of undertaking the dramatization of a simple episode during the on-site visit. Even a short written task can be elevated from what might otherwise be just another school exercise, by the stimulus of the site. By extension, the possibilities of conjuring up a mental picture of the Stone Age family, seated around their cooking fire, are likely to be enhanced if one attempts such a creative exercise in the stimulating environment of Skara Brae, rather than in the school classroom.

Who makes up the directives?

Ideally, work directives are best made up by the teacher of the class for whom they are intended. Provided that he or she is sufficiently familiar with the place to be visited, there is every advantage to be gained from having them prepared in accordance with current class studies and related to the particular aptitudes and interests of those for whom they are intended.

Many work directives are, however, made up by museums, usually operating through their schools museum services. Understandably, since they are not tailored to the specific needs of any particular class, it is unlikely that they will be universally suitable, especially in terms of what is included and what is left out. Nevertheless, the schools museum officer has often an expertise and an awareness of what pupils are able to do in the context of the museum that the teacher could not be expected to have. Because of this, the ideal arrangement is probably one where there is liaison between museum staff on the one hand and school staff on the other.

Ideally, too, work directives should be graded in terms of age and ability, in order that the maximum benefit be obtained from their use. This complicates the organization, and the net anticipated educational gain must therefore be set off against the additional work involved. Luton Museum is one example of a centre which has produced stimulating and attractive work material for a number of age ranges; another is the Imperial War Museum, which caters for different stages, making available a variety of single sheet question-naires and topic sheets on both World Wars, as well as an attractive illustrated questionnaire for younger children on the theme of the First World War.

Thus, with schools and schools museum services both accepting responsibility for the compilation of work directives, there is a fair variety of format, and a range of reflected interests and ideas of what is desirable. Some are very much 'treasure-hunt' style question-naires—good fun and, given the correct circumstances, perfectly valid and acceptable. Others are concerned to probe deeper and to invite the pupil to extend his investigation beyond the relatively simple processes of identification and classification. Such elements are likely to be included but analysis is also required, and responses to questions which begin with 'How?' and 'Why?' Some are slanted in such a way as to emphasize the acquisition or application of cognitive skills, seeing the museum as in the nature of a quarry. Others may invite the pupil to admire, and perhaps select his 'favourite' exhibit, so laying stress on the affective aspects of experi-ence, seeing the place as less of a quarry and more of an Aladdin's cave. Some directives are plain, some coloured, some have drawings and sketches, some have neither. Most are plainly titled, while others are headed in a style designed to stimulate the interest of young visitors. Warrington Museum, for example, has a rather fetching directive headed, 'Have fun with the Romans in the Museum'! In some instances, the tasks required of the children lay greater emphasis on literary than on artistic response; in others the reverse applies.

All this indicates the plethora of styles which can be found in work directives. As in most things, experience usually brings refine-ment, and this is nowhere better demonstrated than in the first-class productions of the Geffrye Museum in London. For years, and long before the idea was taken up by others, this enterprising institution has produced a varied assortment of work directives for the use of visiting groups of schoolchildren. These take the form of study notebooks as well as worksheets and they are comprehensive and stimulating when used in conjunction with the museum material.

Practical aids to recording

The mechanics of recording also needs to be taken into account. If children are to use work directives, then they need something to write with and something to lean on. Museum custodians take a poor view of school parties using glass-topped display cases as writing desks. The unsatisfactory alternative is to use the floor, but what of the situation at a castle site or an abbey ruin, where there is nothing but the great outdoors? For this reason each child should carry a clip board in which the worksheet can be placed and on which he can write or sketch. These can be purchased at office stationers, but many schools improvise quite effectively with a piece of stiff card and a bulldog clip. Some museums issue clip boards on a loan basis to visiting school parties, but one should not assume this, and should always check in advance. A few (e.g. Ipswich, the Victoria and Albert and the National Army Museums) also issue folding stools, a facility which adds to the comfort of a working visit and helps to improve the quality of the written work.

As to the shape and size of work directives, this is a matter for personal preference, but for practical purposes some simple guide lines are worth bearing in mind. In the first place, they should be of a manageable size; something like 25.5 x 20 cm is recommended as being sufficiently large to allow for the presentation of a reasonable amount of material, without producing any handling difficulty. If the intention is subsequently to incorporate completed sheets in a loose-leaf work book, such as might be used by a pupil engaged in a project study, then obviously the page size of the work book will determine that of the directive. This, of course, would only apply where the class teacher was making up his own material. The local museum, however accommodating it might be in any number of respects, could not be expected to tailor its work directives to a size that every participating school would consider suitable.

The length of the visit

Nothing has been said about the length of directives; again, this is a matter for personal choice. The age and interests of the pupils and the character of the place being visited are determining factors. Perhaps it is better to think in general terms and, having decided how long the visit is to be, determine how much of that time is to be spent on directive work. One thing which has to be avoided is the temptation to try to see everything on the one visit. The result can so often be counter-productive, with pupils mentally and physically exhausted by the end of the day. Selectivity, coupled with good planning and preparation is a surer formula for success. A commonly accepted visiting time is about an hour and a half, with allowance (perhaps a quarter of an hour) for time at the sales stall. Implicit in what has just been said is the notion that not all of the time of the visit will be spent on directive-based work. To return to a point made at the beginning of this chapter, there is a time when work directives are appropriate and another when they are not. There is also a time when the simpler study guide is probably more relevant to the situation. It is best, however, that it should not be seen as a matter of simple alternatives. There may be occasions when a study guide can be used in conjunction with a directive, the one perhaps preceding the other. In the same way, the directive could occupy only a part of the visiting time, with the rest given over to just looking at what is there. One has to remember that between a situation where there is total commitment of visiting time to work directives, and one in which there is a complete absence of any kind of directive work, there lies a range of possibilities. Most wise teachers will recognize this and adapt their procedures accordingly.

Let us suppose that a school party is taken for the first time to visit the Science Museum in South Kensington. It is the kind of museum where directed study could most profitably be organized. On the other hand, the whole place is so manifestly attractive for children, that it would certainly be appropriate to limit the formal work and allow opportunity for just looking at and savouring the 'magic' of the exhibits. The Children's Gallery alone is well worth programming in this way. Depending on the nature of the group, the informal part could be organized either as a simple conducted tour or as a free browse, and could just as easily precede as follow any formal work being undertaken. In certain circumstances it could even be an advantage to split the total visiting time in half and thereby have two groups alternating on directed work and a general walk round. Such an arrangement is obviously feasible and practical when there are two supervising teachers; when the teacher is alone, it could still work, but only if the pupils were sufficiently responsible to be left to undertake the tour on their own, while the teacher remained available for consultation on the directed work.

In conclusion, however much we may recognize that the basic function of study guides or work directives is to help bring young people to an awareness of the significance of what they see, these aids should never be allowed to become ends in themselves. Their function is to contribute towards the success of the visits, the principal purpose of which is to look and enjoy. Properly handled, there is no reason why they should not help to ensure the maximum educational gain consistent with those primary objectives.

5
Compiling a Work Directive

Many of these points can perhaps be more effectively illustrated by examining in detail an actual worksheet and considering the reasons for the inclusion of the items as well as the purpose behind the wording of directions and questions. There follows a brief consideration of a work directive prepared for pupils in a Glasgow secondary school. The theme which the class was undertaking was concerned with the Victorian period. Because of this it seemed appropriate to consider the possibilities of using local museum material, and in particular the resources of the Old Glasgow Museum, a compact institution housed in a building of three floors and within which the exhibits were conventionally arranged in traditional glass cases. In terms of category, the institution was essentially a small folk museum, but owing to the paucity of early material was slanted fairly strongly towards the late eighteenth and nineteenth centuries. At the time of our visit, the Museum possessed none of the advantages, in respect of layout, of such comparable museums as Newarke Houses in Leicester and it was certainly not in any significantly active sense involved in work with schools, as was the case with places like the Geffrye or London Museums. There was no sales stall literature, not even an official guide book to the exhibits, but it was a fairly fruitful source of Victoriana, and this was what was wanted. (The Museum has since had a complete face-lift under a new curator, and is now most active with the Schools Museum Service.)

An initial visit showed that the Victorian material was scattered throughout almost every section of the Museum, and clearly this was going to make the task of constructing a worksheet more difficult. On the other hand, from an organizational point of view, the arrangement was potentially advantageous in terms of the visit itself, because a visiting class could be split up among the scattered exhibits in such a way as to prevent overcrowding at any one point. This being the situation envisaged, it was necessary to consider the appropriateness of designing a work directive which could be begun at a number of alternative starting points so that, although ultimately all the pupils would complete the entire exercise, each small group of children would tackle the sections in a different order.

The first section determined on was 'Costume', as there were Victorian items among the dress exhibits. Nothing can stimulate the imaginative reconstruction of the past more effectively than a look at what people actually wore, either for everyday use or for special occasions. A second section was entitled 'Curiosities', an eclectic grouping of items with the single common factor that each one helped to shed light on certain Victorian social customs. 'Scientific invention' was seen as of sufficient importance to merit treatment in a special section, the more especially since Lister did so much of his best work during the time (1860–69) that he was Professor of Surgery at Glasgow University. A fourth section, entitled 'Characters and Closes' was compiled in order to draw attention towards the appearance of the streets and tenement dwelling houses that made up much of the poorer housing of this great nineteenth-century industrial city. Along with this were items concerned with some of the familiar street characters of the time, who either traded, begged or entertained the public at large. Finally a section entitled 'Home sweet Home' was so designed as not only to highlight the nature of the interiors of those poor houses but also to illuminate the divisions in society by contrasting them with the more opulent homes of the Victorian middle class.

The work directive is headed as follows:

School _ _ _ _ _ _ _ _ _ Pupil's name _ _ _ _ _ _ _ _ _ Class _ _ _ _ _ _ _

Old Glasgow Museum   Victorian Glasgow   Work directive 1

Ground floor left: Costume

(In this section, do *either* Questions 1–4 *or* Questions 5–8)

The directive carries at the head proper identification both of the subject and of the pupil undertaking the investigation. The section is also clearly indicated, coupled with the broad location of the relevant items. In this last respect, there is no particular advantage in concealing from the children the whereabouts of any exhibit which one wishes them to examine, hence the inclusion of room directions. It may well be that the presence of an exhibit or group of exhibits is so obvious as to make direction unnecessary. On the other hand, to leave out instructions of this kind in situations where they are needed is to waste time and invite confusion and possibly even frustration among the pupils. It is a different matter if 'treasure-hunting' is initially intended, but if the objectives are more serious every assistance ought to be given to allow the work to begin without delay.

Once the pupils are brought into the correct exhibit area there are advantages to be had from getting them to pick out the required object from the full collection on display. In homing on to one particular exhibit they have to subject others to a process of elimination and in doing this they probably become more generally aware of the nature of the collection than would otherwise be the case. Analysis and elimination of this kind is in itself a valid historical exercise.

The opening section of the worksheet begins with a set of questions on a Victorian wedding dress, with an alternative group on army uniform.

1. *Find the 1886 wedding dress.*
   Write a description of it, as if for a fashion magazine.
   (Mention bodice shape and style, neck-line, bustle, draped
   overskirt, contrasting cuffs, material used.)

As in all questions, adequate space is left for answers to be written in below. On the matter of the content of the questions, the request is simply for a piece of descriptive recording, and this is always a perfectly acceptable type of item for a work directive, provided opportunities are also given on the sheet for the exercise of other skills. In this case the item is also drafted in such a way as to elicit a full answer: the invitation to the pupil to imagine that he or she has been asked to submit a short account to a fashion magazine is intended to act as a stimulus to the imagination. The suggestions included in the bracketed note should help to ensure that responses, which in some instances might be fairly bald and incomplete, are perhaps rounded out to a greater extent than they might otherwise be. To do this is not to undertake the pupils' work for them, but simply to offer some simple supportive guidance which stops short of providing an answer but perhaps makes all the difference to its final quality.

2. *What is one of the main differences between this wedding dress and the dress which a bride of today would be most likely to wear for a church wedding?*

The pupils are then asked to identify a major difference between the dress in the case and one which a modern bride would be most likely to wear to church. Now despite the greater degree of informality which in recent years has affected a range of social customs, not least those associated with weddings, it is still likely that most pupils would recognize that the traditionally accepted colour of the modern bride's dress is white. The wedding dress in the case, dating from 1886, was made up for a Mrs McMeechan of Newton Mearns and is grey in colour. This time, the question is worded in such a way that the pupil has to go beyond straight observation and recording and reflect upon a major point of contrast. This is not to say that the question is a particularly difficult one. It could in fact have been put in an even simpler manner, for example, 'How does the colour of this wedding dress differ from that of most modern ones?' Nevertheless, it invites the exercise of a particular historical skill that goes beyond plain recorded description.

The specific way in which the item is worded also raises the matter of pupil response to open-ended questions. In this case children are asked not simply to comment on the main difference between this and a modern wedding dress but also, initially, to identify that difference. There is every possibility that some pupils might select a totally different feature from the one which the compiler had in mind. Thus although many modern brides' dresses are fashioned in such a way as to incorporate Victorian features in the design, some pupils might still feel that the draped skirt or the bustle were sufficiently unusual to constitute the 'main difference' highlighted by the question. Others, skilled, or at least interested, in needlecraft might focus attention on the fact that, whereas the modern dress is usually a machine-made garment, the Victorian one has obviously been hand sewn. Bearing in mind the nature of historical interpretation, a variety of responses is something which one has to accept and, in many cases, even encourage. To assume that there must always be pupil consensus with what the compiler regards as the 'correct' answer, would be to reduce an otherwise intellectual and imaginative historical exercise to the level of an IQ test.

3. *Unlike many modern garments, Victorian clothes were made to last for a long time. A special dress like this would also have been very expensive to make. How do these two facts help us to understand why the Victorian bride had her wedding gown made up in the style of a dinner dress?*

This is a more difficult question than the previous two. One would hope that the facts, as presented, i.e. that the dress was both expensive and meant to last, would perhaps lead the children to attempt to produce a logical hypothesis, such as, that it was the lady's intention after her marriage to adopt the dress for regular wear. Indeed, it was a recognized custom, and Mrs McMeechan, the bride, who lived in a good residential area and was in all probability from a prosperous household, is still likely to have wished to follow that practice. Since the children are told in the question that the style is that of a dinner dress, they can probably deduce its future use.

4. *Draw the dress in the space provided, and underneath write, 'Wedding dress 1886'.*

An opportunity is now given to the pupils to make a simple sketch of the dress. One would estimate that in this instance the pupil would need no preliminary help with the drawing, so that provision of a space is all that is required. The wording of the item makes it explicitly clear that this is the purpose of the space otherwise some pupils might attempt to execute the drawing elsewhere.

In drafting these opening four items, the compiler was concerned to present tasks which it was reasonable to assume the pupils would be able to tackle. Where it was felt that additional information was required, it was supplied, for example in the first two sentences of item 3. On the other hand, unreasonable questions were avoided. It would, for example, have been possible to ask, 'How many yards of material do you think went into the making of this dress?' but pupil answers in such an instance would be likely to be products of guesswork. Again, one might enquire as to how they dry-cleaned such dresses in the days before the proliferation of establishments specializing in that service, but it would be quite unreasonable to expect a modern child to know about the cleansing properties of fuller's earth.

Four alternative questions on the theme of 'Costume' focus attention on the 1870–74 uniform of the 19th Lanarkshire Rifle Volunteers (HLI), a sort of precursor of the Territorial Army.

5. *Find the 1870–74 uniform of the Lanarkshire Rifle Volunteers. Write a description of it, just as you would if you were writing about it in a short history of the regiment. (Mention colour and shape of doublet, the tartan trews, leather bandolier, silver belt, sword strap and swagger cane.)*

This splendid Victorian uniform is that of an officer, and is a most colourful affair. It consists of a doublet in Rifle Green, trews of Breadalbane Campbell tartan, a bandolier in black leather with embroidered silver thread and silver clasps, a matching belt and a silver-topped swagger cane. The sword strap hangs in a long loop at the left.

This is essentially the same kind of question as was asked in connection with the wedding dress, i.e. descriptive recording. In this case, too, a list of suggestions to assist the compilation is included in brackets.

6. *What is one of the main differences between this uniform and the kind which a local Territorial Army soldier in the Parachute Regiment would wear today?*

It is reasonable to assume that most pupils will be acquainted with the style of a modern soldier's uniform. Even if personal contact is unknown, many model toys, such as *Britain's Models* or *Action Man* show such detail, and television and army displays are other regular sources of this kind of information. As with question 2, this goes beyond observation, and directs the pupils to examine points of contrast with something else. Like the other question, it is also to a degree open-ended so that, although the compiler could well have in mind an answer which focused on the colourful nature of the Victorian uniform by contrast with the camouflaged denim of a modern soldier, it is more than likely that some pupils would find other perfectly valid points of contrast, such as the tighter cut of the Victorian garments or the difference in the nature of the small arms that were borne.

7. *Why do you think that nowadays this uniform would be considered as quite unsuitable for modern combat conditions?*

This is an exercise in deduction, and an extension of the previous question. Any suggestion that the worksheet compiler might be attempting to compare different things, and that the Victorian officer's uniform was essentially for ceremonial rather than functional purposes, is negated by the evidence that soldiers of the time did go into action dressed in this way. Furthermore, right up to and well into the First World War, it was not unknown for subalterns to advance on the enemy armed with little more than a cane of the type displayed in the case. One would hope that the pupil would be able to see the unsuitability for battle of a uniform that was so obvious as to be easily picked out, and so tight as to restrict the kind of movement that might be necessary in an emergency. The ultra-fine decoration, unlikely to stand up to much rough usage such as lying on the ground, and the absence of effective firearms would also be points worthy of comment.

8. *Draw the uniform in the space up above, and underneath write '1870–74 Lanarkshire Rifle Volunteers (HLI): Officer's uniform'.*

It should be noted that in this and in question 4, the pupil is asked to caption the drawing concerned.

Again, as with the questions on the wedding dress, the intention is to avoid the inclusion of anything that might be regarded as unreasonable. Thus, 'What would the officer have carried in the bandolier?' would simply invite guesses, as would, 'Name another famous Volunteer regiment of this time'. There is a time and place for finding these things out, but probably at the follow-up stage, when the information gleaned in the museum and the deductions made therefrom, can be used as a base from which to extend the pupil's knowledge of the theme being pursued.

The next section of the worksheet is concerned to direct the pupil's attention towards a number of objects of an unusual or distinctive type. Three have been chosen and, for want of a better all-encompassing label, have simply been called 'Curiosities'. In each example an illustration is provided as a guide to the children in finding the items.

Ground floor centre: Curiosities

9.

(a) *What was this object called?*

(b) *Who would have used it?*

(c) *When and how would he have used it?*

(d) *Can you think of an occasion when he would, perhaps, not have taken time to use it?*

The object to be identified is what was known as a 'tipstaff'. Measuring about 13 cm long, it was a little rod of ebony, with a brass cap at one end and a brass crown at the other. A century ago, a policeman's authority to arrest a suspect was demonstrated by the act of touching the suspect's shoulder with this diminutive baton. The modern equivalent would be that of a policeman showing his warrant card. In the museum, the information required for answering (a), (b) and (c) can be had from the ticket which accompanies the item. The purpose of (d) is to get the children thinking a bit beyond this, by inviting them to offer suggestions as to when the use of the tipstaff would, perhaps, be inappropriate. Such, for example, would obviously be the case at the culmination of a chase after a thief who had been caught in the act.

10. *Look for the object shown in the illustration, which is a Royal Sovereign knife cleaner of about 100 years ago.*

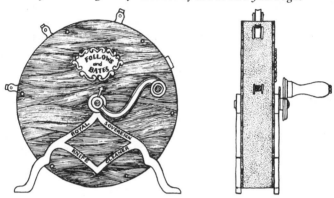

Notice that there are three small apertures on the side of the apparatus, into which the knife blades would have been inserted.

(a) Look into any one of those apertures, and write down what you see.

(b) Having discovered this information, can you suggest what happened inside the round wooden box, as the handle was turned?

(c) When the knife cleaner was about to be used, the large round plug on the side was removed, so that something could be put into the machine to assist the cleaning process. If you had to use the knife cleaner today, what would you put into this opening?

The ornate brass plate on the handle side of this interesting relic of Victorian kitchen hardware tells us that the 'Royal Sovereign Knife Cleaner' was a product of the firm of Follows and Bates. A curved handle operated on a central axis, to cause the rotation of sets of brushes within the circular shaped wooden case. Three apertures were available for the insertion of the knife blades and in each case there was a short, external protruding piece, against which the knife handle rested firmly during the operation of the cleaning process. Cleaning powder was inserted through a plug hole in the side.

In this question, the pupil is encouraged to study the item and, we hope, to note the solidity of it and the magnificently carved brass trade plate on the front. With (a) and (b) he is given a little prompting, and encouraged to find out how the thing worked. Section (c) of the question then builds upon this with a little additional prompting, in order to elicit more thought on its operation.

The point about this question is that we are doing the next best thing to having the pupil actually work the machine. We are leading him, step by step, to a close examination of it, primarily directed towards discovering how it operated. We might instead have asked him to, 'Write down the name of the machine', or 'Say where it was made', but there would not have been a great deal of purpose in doing so. The next question probes a little further, and is concerned to draw out the reasons why we no longer require things like this.

11. *In the days when this was used regularly, there was certainly a need for it, because knife blades tended to become badly stained and marked by such substances as vinegar, sauce and even water. In the light of this knowledge, can you suggest why present-day cutlery does not usually have to be put into a machine of this kind?*

Of course, we are trying to produce the response that whereas modern cutlery is 'stainless', Victorian was not. Those occasions, 100 years ago, when the family dinner included an application of mint sauce to the roast lamb meant a major cutlery cleaning job afterwards!

The last question on this item then explores the social implications, again offering a little information.

12. *Can you think of two reasons why a machine of this kind is more likely to have been found in the larger and wealthier middle-class homes, than in the homes of working-class people?*

Obviously, the cost of the machine would have been a significant factor, and pupils might be able to draw on their own knowledge of how difficult it is to purchase labour-saving devices out of household budget expenses. Perhaps they even need to be told that the

Victorians did not know much about the modern British institution of 'hire purchase'. One would hope that pupils would also be able to make deductions about the greater need of a large middle-class household, with family and servants and lots of cutlery used regularly at mealtimes.

13.

Find 'leerie's lantern', which is drawn alongside. Write a description of it beneath the drawing. Then,

(a) Write down what leerie's job was
(b) Say why you think that he needed a lantern like this?

There is a famous poem about a 'leerie' by Robert Louis Stevenson. Perhaps you may have an opportunity of finding it and writing it into your work book when you are back at school.

The first thing the pupil has to do—and the information is available on the exhibit ticket—is to find out the meaning of the term 'leerie'. In fact, it was the commonly applied description of a lamplighter at a time when the streets and tenement stairs were lit by gas. In those days, the leerie would have had to carry a small ladder, as well as his lantern. The lantern was to help him find his way around the streets and dark stairways as well as ignite the gas, and the ladder was to assist him to climb up the lamp standards. The question is designed to direct children's attention to a person who would have been as common a sight on the city streets as the postman and who, like the postman, would have passed by their doors, twice every day. It was this which so inspired Stevenson to write his nostalgically evocative poem about the lamplighter of Howard Place, Edinburgh:

My tea is nearly ready and the sun has left the sky;
It's time to take the window to see Leerie going by:
For every night at teatime and before you take your seat,
With lantern and with ladder he comes posting up the street.

Unlike the knife cleaner, this is not an exhibit to be dissected but rather something to be looked at and enjoyed, as a direct link with the hissing gas-lit streets of Victorian Glasgow.

The section of the worksheet which follows is called 'Scientific invention'. The main interest must obviously lie in Lister's spray, but there are also opportunities to look at some of the popular optical devices which provided entertainment at the time. Considering that it was a period of many-sided scientific discovery, it is hardly surprising that scientific toys were also produced.

Centre floor right: Scientific invention

14. (*a*) *Find the zoetrope (right hand case at end of room). Read the card alongside to find out how it worked. Now describe below, in your own words, what a viewer would see through the slits as the drum was revolved.*

(*b*) *Complete the drawing by putting in the figures which you can see on the zoetrope in the case.*

This instrument, alternatively named the 'Wheel of Life', was a popular optical toy of the mid-nineteenth century. A successor to the stroboscope, it operated on the principle of a rotating drum, with vertical slits and a series of images placed around its inside surface. Each picture was, in turn, slightly different from the preceding one, so that when the drum was rotated the images were seen by a viewer in rapid succession through the slits in the side. The result was an impression of movement. Favourite subjects were somersaulting clowns, dancers and leaping horses.

This is an example of an item which one really needs to see in action in order to appreciate how it worked. The fact that it is inside a glass case and inaccessible makes it necessary to settle for something less, but the purpose of Question 14 (*b*) is to draw attention to how the successive images (in this case, a circus clown jumping through a hoop held by another clown) underwent the kind of change which produced the effect of movement when the drum was rotated. The principle can easily be tried out back at school, by simply drawing a series of gradually changing pictures in the top corners of an old paperback book. When the book is held in one hand, and the pages are rapidly flicked over with the thumb of the other, the result will be an impression of movement, similar to that obtained by the operator of the zoetrope.

15. *There is another interesting optical toy to be found in the case (see diagram). It is called a stereoscope. It is positioned behind the glass of the case, in such a way that you can look through the two eye pieces at the pictures which are held in its frame. Do this, and describe the effect in the space below.*

The simultaneous viewing through the lenses of a pair of photographs, identical in all respects save that they were originally taken from slightly different angles, presents the viewer with a three-dimensional image. The placing of the exhibit in a manner that offers an opportunity to try it out is too good a chance to miss, and it is interesting to note how this makes unnecessary much of the explanation that would otherwise be required were the exhibit not so accessible.

16. *Find Lister's spray*

(a) *Study the exhibit and the account of how it worked, which you will find fully explained on the card along-side. Having done this, write in the correct places the names of the parts as given in the list below.*

Acid jar	*Fuel container*	*Spray outlet*
Steam boiler	*On/off tap*	*Carrying handle*
Heating lamp	*Steam escape valve*	

(b) *Now write down who Lister was, and why he was famous*

The prime intention here is to get the pupil thinking about the mechanical operation of the antiseptic spray, and to do so by looking at the exhibit and reading the information supplied on the accompanying ticket. Some kind of basic comprehension is necessary in order to complete the eight labelling tasks. Full understanding, however, depends on demonstration or experiment, and this can easily be arranged. Referring back to the diagram for a moment, the principle of operation was that steam was driven upwards from the boiler, through the top of the contraption, along a horizontally placed metal tube and out into the air. As the steam passed the small T-junction, from which a rubber tube passed downwards into a glass bottle of carbolic acid, the difference in pressure that was created caused acid to be drawn up the rubber tube and expelled from the apparatus as a fine spray. This was directed over the patient, the instruments, the furniture, the surgeon and the nurses. By cutting a small hole in the side of a milk straw and inserting another piece of straw at right angles to the first piece the principle can be quite simply demonstrated by placing the short, downward length in a glass of water and blowing through one end of the cross-piece.

Incidentally, it would have been possible to ask pupils to do the drawing itself as well as label the parts. In the writer's experience, however, this is a difficult piece of apparatus for pupils to get right and yet, if it is to mean anything, it has to be correctly recorded. That is why labelling alone is preferred.

The next section boasts the unintentionally alliterative title of 'Characters and Closes'. The references are, first, to the colourful characters who were well known in the streets of Glasgow in the period with which the work directive is concerned; most big cities of the time could have produced a comparable selection. The term 'close' is a rather indigenous one, referring specifically to the entrances to those high-storeyed and very crowded tenement buildings which characterized late-nineteenth-century Glasgow. These were the houses of the poor, and they are well represented in a selection of framed photographs which, dating from 100 years ago when photography was in its infancy, are part of the famous Annan collection. The points of reference for the 'characters' are a double row of hung prints, each with appropriate explanatory captions. The four questions at the beginning of this section are undemanding, but they direct attention to a side of the social scene which would have been very familiar to those who lived in the city at that time.

Top floor left: 'Characters and Closes'

17. *What did 'Penny-a-yard' sell?*

Edward Findlay, better known as 'Penny-a-yard', pursued the unusual occupation of making and selling ornamental chain for ladies' dresses. His trading street cry got him his nickname. Children can find this information on a card alongside the print which depicts 'Penny-a-yard' holding out his wares for sale.

18. *From the information available, can you complete this old couplet about one of the 'characters' shown in the gallery?*

> *Rab Haw, the Glasgow . . .*
> *Ate his shirt, but left the button*

This needs no great stretch of imagination to complete because, quite apart from the caption information, the print itself clearly points to the fact that Robert Hall, who lived in the mid-nineteenth century, must have been well known for his enormous size. In truth, he was a celebrated glutton, renowned locally for his large and unselective appetite.

19. *How do you think 'The Teapot' got his nickname?*

The print is of a newspaper seller of the period, standing in characteristic pose, left hand on hip, right hand offering a paper to the next customer. This is an amusing one and popular with the children.

20. *Who was the street performer who threw a wooden ball into the air and caught it in a cup strapped to his forehead? (The apparatus he used is preserved in one of the cases.)*

This is the least demanding of all four questions on the 'characters'. The purpose is simply to lead the pupils to note the man's name (Old Malabar) and then study the exhibit and associated news cuttings about his skilful performance.

Following this, attention is directed to the Annan photographs:

21. *Study the selection of photographs on the stand in the centre of the room. They are of Glasgow closes and backcourts of 100 years ago. Use the evidence of the photographs to write below two or three sentences about the living conditions of the people shown in them.*

The half-dozen or so large photographs are an excellent source of information because they show clearly the twin features of unplanned building and overcrowding that were characteristic of the housing of the tenement slum-dwellers. The intention is that, by a close study of them, a pupil may be able to acquire an insight into the general degradation in which many of the poor then lived. The open drains, communal outside lavatories, shored-up buildings, lack of sunlight, and generally impoverished appearance of the place are all clearly discernible in the photographs. Most of the children should be able to pick up points like these, but there is finer detail which they might miss, such as the projecting washing posts with pulley access, or the hoisting hooks at the gable tops. To get round this the teacher may have to decide whether or not to include one or two simple hints of the kind which accompanied the opening questions on the costume items. In this case such hints are not included, because noting the finer detail was not considered to be as important as acquiring the general impression of what life must have been like for those whose unhappy lot it was to live in such places.

This takes us up to the final section of the work directive, which is centred upon two room layouts, one of which is a poor family's single-roomed house of the type which was very common in the overcrowded tenements of the time. The other is a middle-class Victorian parlour, typically overcrowded with furniture that shows a remarkable combination of opulence and discomfort.

Top floor right: 'Home Sweet Home'

Study the two rooms laid out in this section of the museum

22. *One of these layouts would have been called a 'single-end'; this meant a house complete in itself but of only single-room size.*
    Say which of the two rooms shown here best deserves this description, and give your reasons.

It is evident that the Victorian parlour was in no way multi-functional in the sense alluded to by the question. The other room, however, shows the chairs on either side of the open-range fire, the steel sink with the swan-neck faucet at one side and the recessed bed at the other. Clearly it combined the features of living-room, dining-room, kitchen and bedroom. This was where the family lived, and in situations where it was a large one, the squalor, in some cases, can only be imagined. The main features should be apparent to pupils.

23. *You will notice that the parlour is lit by gas mantles.*
    How do you think the other room may have been lit?

This question is intended to draw attention to the fact that there was a time when gas lighting, like all new inventions, started out in a limited way, with consequent benefits that were not immediately available to all. One would hope that the children would be able to respond, by suggesting the probability of paraffin lamps or candles as the possible sources (if any) of illumination. The presence of candlestick holders in the room should help them to come to conclusions on this.

24. *Beds of the kind seen in the kitchen were known as 'box*
    beds'. Can you say why?

The recessed bed, characteristic of tenement dwellings, where it was an adjunct to the living area, was often closed off by wooden doors during the day. Even in the absence of such discreet camouflage, the fact that it was set into a square recess, and thus walled in on three sides, was enough to suggest the name. Children can deduce this for themselves.

25. *Iron 'door tickets' were fixed to the front doors of tenement*
    houses, stating the area of the house in cubic feet and, for
    health reasons, the number of people who were permitted
    to stay there. What information can you get from the door
    ticket of this house?

Under a local Police Act of 1866, only a certain number were allowed to live in the tenement houses. This laudable legislation was

clearly designed to prevent overcrowding, with consequent health
hazards. In order to guarantee
observance of the law, houses
were 'ticketed', that is to say, an
iron disc was fixed to the outside of the door, stating the
cubic footage of the house and
the number of adults permitted
to live in it. In this instance (see

illustration), the children should be able to deduce that the house
area was 1100 cubic feet and that the accommodation was regarded
as fit for a maximum of 2½ adults. The presence of a rocking cradle
in the middle of the floor should help to resolve any difficulties as to
how to interpret ½ adult.

26. *By comparing and contrasting the two rooms, how much do
you think we can learn about the differences between rich
and poor, 100 years ago?*

This is an open-ended exercise, but having looked previously in
detail at the highly functional nature of the single-roomed house, the
parlour will, by contrast, appear all the more strange. Here one finds
the horse-hair sofa, the bell-shaped glass cases protecting artificial
flowers or stuffed birds, the table with the velvet tasselled cover and
the absence of any suggestion that the room might have served any
purpose beyond that of rest and relaxation. There is much to compare and contrast, not simply in the layout, but in the quality of the
furnishings and the degree of use to which they have obviously been
subjected.

*If you have completed your sheet properly and have time to spare,
look through the museum for articles connected with the police,
about 100 years ago. Describe or draw them below.*

This item is not numbered, because it is in the nature of an
optional extra, something inserted for the youngster who is finished
that little bit ahead of the others. The fact that the Museum has a
good collection of helmets, truncheons, bullseye lamps, handcuffs, a
drunk's barrow and a birch makes it a fruitful source of supplementary
investigation.

This completes the detailed analysis of the process of compiling a work directive. Perhaps it is an appropriate point at which to remark that what has been said is a product of the author's own personal views as to what might constitute an effective compilation. There is no intention that this model should be regarded as anything other than one of a number of possibilities, and not all those who read it will necessarily agree with the conclusions drawn. Perhaps that is just as well, because in work directives nothing should be more assiduously avoided than a stereotyped formula.

Throughout this and the previous chapter, occasional reference has been made to what are termed 'follow-up' activities. In a way, it is an unfortunate term because it implies an order of events which might well be wholly inappropriate. The fact that it has found its way into regular use in discussions on work directives is the reason why it features here, but it would perhaps be more appropriate to think in terms of 'interrelating' or 'interacting', rather than 'follow-up', because it is probably better to think of the museum visit as complementary to other associated activities, rather than occupying any kind of permanent fixed relationship to them. This would mean that the position of the museum visit or visits in a study scheme would be appropriately determined by the progress of the whole programme. It might come in at the beginning, the middle or the end; it might trigger off fresh ideas and new investigations, supplement others or, in itself, be a follow-up to something which had begun in the classroom.

This said, we can now consider the kind of activities which might 'follow-up' those with which this particular worksheet has been concerned, bearing in mind that they could equally well in their turn have produced the motivation for the museum visit itself. They are grouped according to the five sections of the work directive.

Costume
(a) Relating the 1886 dress to preceding and following fashion in order to note detailed change; extending this study as far as is considered desirable.
(b) Investigating uniform styles of other regiments of the time; distinguishing, perhaps, between characteristically different styles of cavalry and infantry regiments, and relating the design

of the 1870—74 uniform to those which preceded and those which followed.

Curiosities
(a) Building up a short dramatic episode round the elaborate formal procedure of arresting a suspect with a tipstaff.
(b) Using the knife cleaner as a starting point for finding out about other Victorian kitchen utensils and devices.
(c) Following up the suggestion regarding R. L. Stevenson's poem on 'The Lamplighter', and writing it out in full.

Scientific inventions
(a) Setting the zoetrope in its correct context, as one of the fore-runners of the motion picture, by investigating also praxino-scopes, kaleidoscopes, magic lanterns, and perhaps making a simple thaumatrope.
(b) Testing the principle of stereoscopic vision by a number of simple experiments. For example:
  1. In holding up a book, edge on, about 15 cm away from the eyes, noting what can be seen when each eye is covered in turn.
  2. In holding up a finger, about 45 cm from the eyes, noting how focusing on the finger produces an impression of double vision in background objects while conversely, focusing on those same background objects produces a similar effect in respect of the finger.
  3. Noting the flat effect of the landscape when seen through one eye only.
(c) Experimenting, as suggested, to discover the principle of Lister's spray.
(d) Using the information on Lister as a starting point for a brief look at other medical discoveries of the period.

Characters and Closes
(a) Extending the enquiry into local 'characters' of the time.
(b) Finding other photographs of the city of the same time as those referred to in the work directive and using them to round out the picture of life at the time.

'Home Sweet Home'

Having examined domestic conditions, following this up by looking at the situation in factories and workshops of the time. Perhaps also finding out about school conditions and how classes of over 100 sat in rows in galleried rooms, chanting arithmetical tables in unison, undertaking the most elaborate problems of mental arithmetic and writing on slates.

6

Schools Museum Services

So far our main concern has been with the part which the school can play in the initiation and direction of activity involving the use of the museum or historical site. The complementary aspect which has to be considered is the extent to which museums and places of historical interest are themselves geared to assist school-based activity. In this respect, the various schools museum services are the most prominent and important supportive agencies, and teachers intending to make use of local facilities would do well to investigate the possibilities of drawing on the valuable help which a well run schools museum service can offer.

The scope and character of such a service varies from one locality to another. Much depends on the nature of the museum and whether its particular emphasis is on a comprehensive, specialist or folk collection. It is also common to find that a schools museum service, though based in one place may operate through a number of museums coming under the jurisdiction of a particular local authority. There is no doubt, however, that the scope of the services in current operation varies enormously. Some are outstanding and their work is thoroughly diversified. The Victoria and Albert, with its wide range of high-quality activity is a good example. There are others where the service tends to be more specialized, like the Geological Museum, which has educational activity primarily directed towards intramural teaching. Many places have an extensive loan service, some offer none at all, while, in certain cases, there is limited provision, restricted perhaps to the urban area immediately served by the museum.

Loans and lectures, are only two of the ways in which schools museum services give support. The provision of holiday and leisure activities such as are offered by places like the Geffrye Museum or Birmingham Museums is becoming increasingly popular, although, again, it is by no means yet established as standard practice. As noted in a previous chapter, supply of information sheets and work directive material is a feature of many museums, but there are others where this service is not offered. The same applies to field study excursions, assistance with projects, in-service teaching and other forms of help. Nor is the size of the museum necessarily a pointer to the nature of the services offered, for many are markedly influenced by the drive and particular enthusiasms of their curators.

Diversity is reflected in the nomenclature given to the organizers of schools museum services so that, in addition to the fairly common title of Schools Museum Officer, one also comes across Schools Liaison Officer, Schools Service Officer, Schools Organizer, Schools Curator, Keeper, Museum Teacher, Museum Education Officer, Extension Services Officer and similar titles.

Loan services

Since the preparation of work directives has already been dealt with, suffice it to say that it is now generally regarded as a recognizable function of schools museum services. The concern of the present chapter is with other aspects, beginning with a consideration of loan facilities.

The practice, on the part of public museums, of lending exhibits to schools is one of long standing and almost all have a loan service of some sort. It was in 1883 that the Reverend Henry Higgins, Chairman of the Museum Sub-Committee for the City of Liverpool, hit upon the idea of organizing what he described as a 'circulating museum'. The effect of this imaginative decision was to make Liverpool the first provincial city in Great Britain to have a museum loan service. Other public museums throughout Britain followed Liverpool's example, but it was a long time before anything in the nature of a formal link was established between a museum operating a loan service and a local education authority. The first was in 1936, when the Derbyshire School Museum Service was set up by the County Education Committee. Since then the idea has grown, until today it is generally regarded as one of the main types of service which a museum ought to provide as part of its educational role in serving the needs of schools. Its principal value is that it facilitates the temporary transfer to schools of material which in normal circumstances would only be available for viewing in the galleries.

Usually, a varied range of exhibits are available on loan, often from the museum's reserve collection, although other types of item that are not strictly speaking *realia* are often classified and issued as part of the loan services. These include art loans, such as framed reproductions of paintings, models, dioramas, maps, films, filmstrips, slides, photographs, tapes and records. Not all museums offering a loan service will necessarily handle such a wide range, but certainly many of them are in a position to be able to offer a good selection of material for borrowing.

However attractive and useful all this may be, from the point of view of the teacher wishing to undertake a particular historical study with a class, the exhibit collection is more likely to be of immediate value. Apart from anything else, the school itself and the local teachers' resource centre could probably between them provide models and audio-visual material, but the provision of exhibit material is likely to be a task which only the museum could discharge effectively. Where possible, museums send original material, but replicas, especially of rare pieces, are also distributed.

Understandably, some places are limited in their available loan material, often because of the relatively small size of the museum's collection; others by contrast, have developed loan facilities over a much wider range. As an example of the latter, Leeds is an authority which has built up a very extensive service, and makes available a good general collection of material, ranging from prehistory to modern times. A page from the Leeds loan catalogue reproduced here shows what is available over a variety of media. Yet even where the collection is a modest one, it is worth remembering that it is possible to find within it specialist groupings of respectable size. Hereford and Worcester County Museum at Hartlebury Castle, for example, is especially strong on Victorian and Edwardian items. Here one finds a very good costume collection of the period, which even includes christening gowns and a crinoline cage. Victorian domestic life is well represented, with a rich array of various intriguing items—a scrapbook, parasols, a polyphone and discs, crimping, goffering and smoothing irons, cameras, and bottles of

Victorian 'pop'. Similarly, the social history section of the loan collection of Hull museum schools service has available a number of fascinating items from the same period, including a sewing machine in full working order, a spinning wheel, a perambulator and a child's two-wheeled 'fan-tail' gig!

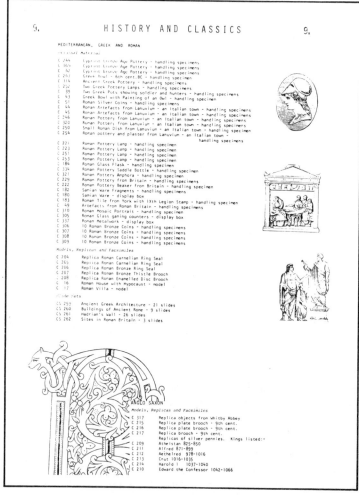

A page from the Leeds City Museum loan catalogue

Consideration of the examples just given immediately raises the question of size of items in loan collections. In fact, actual size exhibits of manageable proportions, whether in original or replica form, are the commonest type. Where the inclusion of a large item in a loan collection would be impossible, it is common for museums to provide model-scale exhibits and to distribute them on the same basis as other loan material. For example, schools in the Portsmouth area can borrow from the City Museums an Elizabethan theatre on the scale of ½ inch to 1 foot, or a carrier's broad-wheeled wagon, c. 1800, on a scale of 1 inch to 1 foot.

Nevertheless, although museum and school staff alike would probably regard exhibit items as the most desirable type of resource, this is not to say that loan collections which are not primarily based upon exhibit material are in any way inferior to those that are. What matters is their relevance to particular situations, so that it would probably be better to think in terms of alternative forms of resources which, according to circumstances, would be equally valid as aids to learning. A good example of this is to be found in the activities of the Commonwealth Institute, whose library and resource centre has a wide range of loan material designed to stimulate interest in the Commonwealth and its peoples, in particular through the examination of associated topics, such as aid and development, race relations and education in multiracial schools. The material which may be borrowed to support a study of such themes does not include museum exhibits in the normally accepted sense. Instead, it comes as printed sources, like books, articles, wall charts and study kits, together with non-print resources, like produce samples, filmstrips and tape recordings. Despite the absence of exhibit type material, the loan scheme of the Commonwealth Institute offers a rich and varied collection, with a good number of the kits specifically concerned with historical themes. Incidentally, it is worth noting that a wide range of material of this kind, which includes also posters, maps and flags, can be purchased as well as borrowed.

Naturally, one thing which can help to determine the size and quality of a loan service is the extent to which the museum is committed in other directions. Some try to cater for all the types of extension services which might be called for, while others prefer, as a matter of policy, to concentrate on fewer services, but to develop those that they have to a greater extent than would be possible if their efforts were diffused. One good instance of this is to be found at Reading. This museum offers no teaching service, but it is particularly strong in its wide-ranging loan collection; a recent development especially worthy of note, is a series of occupational costume figures and child-size replica dress from different historical periods. From the latter, schools are free to borrow both boys' and girls' costumes for late medieval, Puritan and Georgian periods, and boys' clothes for the Tudor period.

How is the loan material distributed? This may vary a great deal from one service to the next. In some areas teachers are expected to collect as well as return their own borrowed material. In other instances, deliveries are made by the museum service to a central distribution point. Increasingly schools museum services are undertaking responsibility for both deliveries and collections, and obviously where such arrangements operate, there is more encouragement to teachers to make the fullest use of the service. In a number of notable cases the details are worked out with a great deal of thought, in order to ensure that the system operates fully and efficiently. For example, Bristol City Museum invites submissions on an application card of the dates on which particular exhibits are required. The normal loan period is a week and this has the effect of encouraging teachers to spread their requests over a term rather than requisition in a single order for all anticipated requirements, only to have a sizeable proportion of it lying unused at any one time. With this information, it is possible for the museum service to work out the delivery dates and to notify schools by means of a circular letter, sent out at the beginning of each term. For organizational purposes the city is divided into five areas, each with a different day for the delivery and collection of material. The co-operation of schools is simply limited to meeting the request that the special cases for transporting the exhibits are packed and made ready for collection by 9.15 a.m. on the morning on which they are due to be returned to the museum.

From the schools' point of view, most loan services operate in a straightforward manner, but some cautionary advice can be offered. To begin with, one has to establish eligibility for borrowing. There is unlikely to be any restriction, but some museums do place limitations on categories of borrowers. The National Museum of Wales, for example, has one of the largest of all loan services, but restricts it to secondary schools, colleges of education and teachers' centres.

Assuming that eligibility to borrow has been established, applications for any kind of listed material should be made well in advance in order to minimize the possibility of disappointment, and this should be done according to the pattern established by the museum in question. In some places this procedure may be fairly informal, but with the larger museums there is likely to be a set pattern which teachers will be expected to follow. When material arrives at the school, it should be carefully checked. There could be an item missing or damaged in transit and, if so, teachers are advised to notify the museum service immediately. Another reason for checking the exhibits on arrival is to note how they were packed. It is always a good idea to pay careful attention to this, even to the extent of making a quick sketch, before removing anything from its packing case or box. The museum staff are likely to be knowledgeable and expert at packing loan material in a way that teachers could not expect to be, so that there is all the more reason for exercising care.

Finally, as regards breakage, it goes without saying that borrowers will endeavour to do everything possible to prevent this from happening. Nevertheless, from time to time accidents do occur and it is as well to know what to do in such an event. The first essential is to recover all the pieces, however minute. A shattered pot, for example, can usually be put together again, provided all the bits are made available to the restorer. Many a museum show case is graced by a beautiful exhibit which was once little more than a pathetic heap of sherds. In the case of pottery, glass, tile or similar vulnerable substances the pieces should be carefully wrapped in soft tissue paper in order to prevent damage to the fine sharp edges of the fragments. The original breakage is most likely to have been the consequence of a simple accident, but carelessly junking the pieces into a box and thus aggravating the damage done would be an inexcusable act of deliberate vandalism. There is one other golden rule concerning breakage: teachers should under no circumstances try to repair damaged items themselves. No matter how slight the damage may be, it is always a job for the expert.

In general, as regards the use of loan services, teachers would do well to review all the possibilities within their own areas. It may well come as a surprise to many to discover what can actually be borrowed. And even if such an exploratory investigation should yield nothing of immediate and apparent relevance to the work in hand it could well be related to other areas of the curriculum, and so indicate possibilities for future borrowing.

Portable exhibitions

Dundee Museum and Art Galleries, in addition to offering the normal extension services of lectures, demonstrations and loans, has a special feature which takes the form of a travelling exhibition. For the most part, it consists of large display panels, on which are mounted a range of visual material, prominent among which is the photographic blow-up; the panels are headed with appropriate captions. Schools may book an exhibition for a two-week display period and, to assist the teacher in undertaking classroom preparation, relevant notes and work directives are available in advance. Successful and popular themes have included 'Grandfather's Schooldays', 'Castles from the Air', and 'Dundee by Gaslight'.

In the case of 'Dundee by Gaslight', forty lantern slides from the museum's collection were made up into enlarged print format for display panel purposes. Each panel had associated notes describing the features of the photograph and was accompanied by questions and suggested activities for children to undertake. The photographs covered the years 1860 to 1914, and showed the transport of the time, including jute and whaling ships, horses and carriages, tramcars and balloons! Costumes of the period, of both rich and poor, were also depicted. In addition supporting displays exhibited material appropriate to the period. Thus, the contemporary 'poet and tragedian of Dundee', William McGonagall was represented, and another case recalled the tragic Tay Bridge railway disaster of 1879, by exhibiting an old carriage door, the number of the engine and various other relics salvaged from the river. Three early bicycles, some street name plates, a mural of the first Tay Bridge, old advertisements and a drunk's barrow completed the exhibition.

Colchester and Essex Museum is another centre which organizes a fairly extensive range of portable exhibitions. They tend to be on a smaller scale than those presented by Dundee, but there are more of them. Many are slanted towards seeing the local story against the background of the broader period. Thus we have such themes as 'Roman Colchester', 'Medieval Colchester', 'Georgian Colchester' and so on. There are fourteen such exhibitions now available for school use, and the latest addition is on the topic of 'Victorian Colchester'; this includes genuine museum exhibits, colour slides, tape recordings, two small dioramas and nine display panels.

The notion of a portable exhibition has particularly commended itself to the schools service of the National Museum of Wales. Traditionally the Museum has always been concerned with the problems of the rural areas, some of which are in mountainous terrain, and over 300 kilometres from the headquarters of the service. Over the last few years, increasing attempts have been made to cater for the needs of schools located in those distant parts, and what has emerged is what its sponsors call the 'museum workshop'. This is, in essence, a temporary exhibition, based partly on items from central and local museums and supplemented by demonstration material; the presentation of a 'workshop' at a convenient local centre in a remote area is aimed at producing the maximum practical response from visiting groups drawn from surrounding schools. Where such presentations are specifically concerned with historical themes, efforts are made to relate them to matters of local interest. For example, the North Wales Quarrying Museum at Llanberis, 270 kilometres away from the Cardiff-based schools museum service was made the temporary centre for demonstrations of quarrying crafts, undertaken in connection with existing museum display. In most cases, the workshop lasts for a week, and schools send parties in turn, according to a pre-arranged timetable. Encouragement is given to children to touch, and even use, exhibits, and suggestions for further practical activity back at school are provided for teachers. It is standard practice also for the 'workshop' to be accompanied by the production and provision for school use of guide leaflets, questionnaires and book lists.

Portable exhibitions can also provide an effective stimulus to activity beyond the limits of one class. Whereas loan collections can be particularly useful for single class groups, there is much to commend the exhibition as suited to the concurrent use of many classes, perhaps even for different purposes. Like the loan collection, however, its principal value lies in the way in which it effectively extends the museum into the school itself, thereby making available much of the benefit of a museum visit, at the same time circumventing many of the practical disadvantages which so often have to be overcome if such a trip is to be successful.

Project work

Help with project work is an obvious function of both loan collections and portable exhibitions, and in this respect many teachers will recognize their most obvious application. Many museums, however, go beyond this servicing function, and assume it to be part of their responsibility to offer active help to teachers and pupils engaged in project work. Some, like Glasgow, in anticipation of this, arrange many of their intramural lecture programmes to match the topics most favoured by schools and most regularly included in curricula. Others are willing to assist in the planning stage of a project and to offer subsequent co-operation by providing special exhibitions and temporary displays. Some will themselves initiate study projects; in Chapter 7 the material from the work of the former London Museum is illustrative of this.

A few museums, like Norwich, encourage children engaged in projects to write to the museum's education officer, in order to seek the use of objects from the reserve collection. Likewise, the Imperial War Museum has produced a leaflet explaining the nature of the help it can offer to children undertaking projects on the two World Wars. However they choose to do it, most museums will be very willing to help with material from their loan collections for either ongoing or follow-up work. It may also be possible, as in Bradford, for certain demonstrations, such as the use of a spinning wheel, to be included where appropriate to the subject being studied. One museum which has made a particular specialism of helping schools with projects is the Geffrye Museum in east London. Founded in 1914, it displays, through a sequence of period rooms, the history of English furniture and decorative arts from 1600 to the present day. Single visits of school parties are accommodated, but provision is also made for schools wishing to arrange a series of visits in order to pursue one or other of a number of themes on offer. Wednesdays are set aside for schools to utilize the full museum facilities in carrying out special projects; both library and art room are available for some of the detailed academic and practical follow-up work that can make such a visit so much more educationally purposeful.

A particularly interesting example of specialist help is to be found in the activity of the Leicestershire Record Office, which is linked to the museums. Here, children are given access to nineteenth- and twentieth-century documents, and work on these original sources has been undertaken by pupils of different age groups. By confining the work to primary sources drawn from a relatively recent historical period, the organizers have been able to avoid the kind of palaeographic difficulties which older material might have presented.

In some cases, the nature of the help offered takes the form of prepared kits. For example, in anticipation of a later visit, Bowes Museum in County Durham issues these to schools well in advance, so that the group can be well prepared. The preparatory kit is handed back when the party visits the museum.

A particularly striking example of study kit production is to be found in the John Judkyn memorial kits, which are constructed around various aspects of North American history. Arising out of an idea first begun in the Children's Museum of Indianapolis, and subsequently developed by the John Judkyn Memorial at Bath in Avon, they have been employed through all levels of formal education, from play school up to university, so demonstrating the appeal which tangible reminders of the past can have for students of all ages. Well over seventy kits are available for hire by schools and their contents are such as to enrich any appropriately linked project. For example, one of the kits on nineteenth-century Negro slavery includes a first edition of *Uncle Tom's Cabin*, a 'servant' tag, a Staffordshire group of 'Uncle Tom and Eva', and slave handcuffs. Of the numerous Judkyn kits on the American Civil War, three consist of dioramas, while others include such items as bayonets, bullets, confederate currency, soldiers' mess tins, boots, spurs and railway tickets. The figure overleaf shows a typical page from the Judkyn kit catalogue.

A study kit need not only be a collection of items for display. In certain circumstances it can also provide a rich source of pupil activity. Worthy of mention in this context are the archaeological study boxes put out for the use of local schools by the Colorado

ALASKA

Kits	A 1 E H	includes: Eskimo bowdrill, harpoon shaft, mask, snow glasses, etc.
	A 2 E H	includes: Eskimo bone game, dressed figure, ivory animals, etc.
	A 3 E H G	includes: Eskimo doll, Aleutian bidarkie, sealskin boot, etc.
	A T1	"Inviting-in" dance song

HAWAII

| Kits | H 1 E H | includes: poi pounder, wooden bowl, tapa beater, etc. |
| | *H 2 H G | includes: ula maika stone, adze, pu ili rattle, contemporary map of Captain Cook's voyages |

THE CIVIL WAR

Kits	*CW D1	Diorama – Union cavalry charging a Confederate gun emplacement.
	*CW D2	Diorama – Federal defending a bridge.
	*CW D3	Diorama – Confederate troops moving into new positions.
	*CW 1 E H G	includes: contemporary photographs, cartridge box, bayonet, bullet mould, etc.
	CW 2 E H G	includes: cavalry boot, spur, curry comb, ramrod head, $10 Confederate bill, etc.
	CW 3 E H G	includes: cavalry boot, contemporary photographs, mess tins, canteen, etc.
	CW 4 H G	includes: spur, shot, bullets, $20 and $10 Confederate bills, newspaper, etc.
		Supplementary Graphic Material
	CW 5 G	includes: Engraving Jefferson Davis, paper currency, contemporary photographs, etc.
	CW 6 G	includes: soldier's railway ticket, paper currency, contemporary photographs, etc.
Books	CW B1	"The Civil War" American Heritage New Illustrated History of the U.S. Volume 8
	CW B2	"American Heritage Picture History of the Civil War" by Bruce Catton
Tapes	CW T1	Music and speeches relating to the Civil War
	CW T2	Music and speeches relating to the Civil War

OPENING OF THE WEST

Kits	WM 1 E H G	includes: Branding Iron, Cinch hook, surveyor's chain, etc.
	* WM 2 E H G	includes: diorama, tethering spike, branding iron, Jefferson medal, etc.
	WM 3 E H	**Spanish America** includes: Retablo, Bulto, Yucca whip, Matraca, Cross, "Jerga", etc.

*Owing to the awkward size of these Kits it is not possible for them to be sent by British Rail.

Extract from catalogue of John Judkyn Memorial Kits

State Museum at Denver. These are lightweight containers, filled either with soil or an effective substitute like dried-out coffee dregs. Planted and hidden in the soil are various archaeological 'finds' and the pupil's task is to literally unearth them, taking the proper care, employing the correct tools and using recognized archaeological techniques. A plastic sheet approximately 2 x 2 metres is supplied to cover the classroom floor. Considering the damage so often done on excavations where enthusiastic amateurs are inadequately supervised, it will be appreciated that a kit of this kind can be not only a display medium but a valuable training resource as well. This Museum also offers project kits of materials relating to the past history of Colorado's ethnic minorities. Items like Sioux beadwork or New Mexican wood carvings have been selected as reflecting the traditions and values that have been preserved from the heritage of each group.

In considering the ways in which museums and sites can aid and support project work, it should be borne in mind that most of those places have a sales stall where items may be purchased at a modest price. Smaller museums or sites usually confine themselves to guide books, postcards and slides. Nevertheless, from the child's point of view this is particularly useful, because most of such items can be bought out of pocket money. A good example is the National Army Museum where coloured postcards of soldiers in uniform are available at only a few pence each. Most are reproductions of paintings, carried out originally either as individual works or as items in a series. Apart from their relevance for certain school-based study themes, many children may simply like to collect them for the same reasons as generations of schoolchildren have always wanted to build up their own collections of things that were attractive to them.

Some of the bigger museums also sell replicas of selected exhibits. It is possible to purchase breastplates, helmets and firemarks at the Castle Museum in York, or jewellery pieces at the Victoria and Albert. The most notable service of this kind is to be found at the British Museum, where a range of variously priced objects are offered. For relatively little expense the Museum makes available replicas of Mesopotamian cylinder seal impressions, or of a cuneiform tablet giving a chapter of the Babylonian 'Epic of Creation'. At the other end of the scale are the more ambitious and expensive items, such as the marble head of the Horse of Selene from the East Pediment of the Parthenon, a sizeable piece of sculpture (53.3 cm high and 87 cm wide) and very beautiful. Although beyond the means of a school, an item of this kind could become a valuable addition to a museum loan collection.

If the contents of the sales stall are sufficiently diverse it should be possible for the teacher to assemble some of the elements of a good resource-based study kit. It may be necessary to exploit the possibilities of a number of associated museums to do this, but the result can be most rewarding, especially if this material is supplemented by privately taken photographs or slides. Indeed, the author undertook this agreeable task a few years ago and, by photographing various outdoor sites, as well as visiting the National Museum in Copenhagen, its annexe at Brede, the Roskilde Ship Museum and the open-air folk museum at Lejre, was able to put together enough material for a school study kit on the Viking period in Denmark. Items included are:

1. Guide to the excavations at Roskilde, with sectional drawings of the reconstructed ships.
2. Three sets of 35 mm slides (privately taken), showing:
   (a) the Roskilde ships and the ongoing work of reconstruction,
   (b) Viking ship finds in places other than Roskilde,
   (c) the reconstructed village at Lejre, with its thatched houses and demonstration areas for the practice of ancient crafts.
3. Set of postcards of Viking material held in the National Museum, Copenhagen.
4. Viking ship model kit by Billing Boats (also available in Britain).
5. Gilt Viking ship brooch from Lillevang, ninth century AD (replica).
6. Thor's hammer of silver from Mandemark, tenth century AD (replica).
7. Seal-shaped brooch in silver from Viking period. Place and date unknown (replica).

Putting the kit together was by no means an inexpensive exercise, but there is no doubt about the value which the end-product has for the enrichment of a history course centred upon the Viking period. While conceding that the superlative quality of the museums concerned was a major factor in making collection possible, it is none-theless true that comparable opportunities do exist for similar tapping of the potential of many British museums.

Intramural teaching

As already indicated, many of our museums offer free private lectures to recognized educational and cultural groups. Where there is such provision, teachers may derive considerable benefit by incor-porating within their courses something which is presented in an attractive way by one who is usually a specialist in the subject. Bristol and Glasgow are two particularly good instances of places where such provision has been brought to the highest professional level. In Bristol, the class, accompanied by its teacher, is accom-modated in the museum 'schools room', a technologically well-equipped presentation area and, following a short talk by the museum specialist concerned, is split up into small groups, to work partly in the schools room and partly in the galleries.

The scope of intramural work programmes available again depends on the individual museum. Some provide a fairly diverse range. Norwich, for example, a place which has tended to lay the main emphasis of its museum work on intramural teaching, offers this service to schools at all ages and levels of ability, and classes are held in any one of three schoolrooms located at the Castle, Stranger's Hall and the Bridewell Museum. Full use is made of the reserve collection of material, and presentations are based on a programme of topics circulated to schools at the beginning of each school year. Some themes, which bear a direct relationship to school curricula, appear with regularity, such as 'Prehistoric Tools and Weapons', or 'The History of the Local Textile Industry'. Each year, too, additional and more unusual topics are included; among these are such subjects as 'The History of Light and Lighting' or 'Brasses and Brass Rubbing'.

In other cases, particularly where the museum itself is a special-ized one, the range may be more restricted in terms of content, although it does not follow that it need be any less liberal in the extent of its provision. For example, the Imperial War Museum now offers an extensive assortment of lecture services, but all within the limited field of warfare since 1914. In the summer term, 1974, these included a number of illustrated talks for ten to sixteen-year-olds on 'Trench Warfare', 'The Home Front 1939–45' and 'Women in Wartime'. Special lectures for sixth form and college groups on such basic themes as 'The Origins of World War II' and 'The Russian Revolution' were also provided, together with film shows, which included 'All Quiet on the Western Front' and 'Cities at War: London 1939–45'.

Of course, the conducting of intramural sessions for schools is not always undertaken exclusively by museum personnel. Some places, in addition to providing intramural lectures conducted by their own staff members, also from time to time organize special lectures by a distinguished expert. Notable examples of this are considered in Chapter 7, in relation to some aspects of the impressive work previously carried out by the schools museum service of the London Museum.

The need for the expert is nowhere more apparent than in the provision of an intramural service of the kind which we are considering, not so much for the school pupils as for the teachers. Several museums are now concerned to make this provision which, broadly speaking, can take one of two forms. The first is the mounting of content courses, designed to provide valuable background and/or revision for a teacher wishing to embark on a particular theme. Prominent in this respect is the Victoria and Albert Museum which has for some time operated a range of three-day courses for teachers on a variety of subjects, such as 'Victorian Daily Life' or 'The Georgians at Home'. Most courses, though not all, are held during vacation time and, as one would expect, the quality is of the highest. They provide excellent opportunities, as much for personal enrichment as for classroom preparation.

The other area in which many museums have a particularly strong interest lies in the arrangement of special courses, for both teachers and students-in-training, on the most suitable ways of using the museum as an aid to teaching. Again, the Victoria and Albert Museum does much in this direction, as do also certain provincial museums, such as Merseyside County, Leicester, Bristol and Ipswich. Here, the purpose is induction into the most effective procedures for conducting school study sessions in association with museums.

In a number of instances guidance for teachers in the techniques of utilizing museums with school classes includes not only instruction in the use of particular museum objects and their display for teaching purposes, but also academic assistance in subject matter. In this way the two kinds of tutorial service are combined. This can, be illustrated by two examples. The first is from the North Western Museum of Science and Industry at Manchester, where an important development has been the organization of courses for teachers in order to familiarize them with those sections of the Museum which they might visit and use with classes. In the case of the 'Textiles' course, this has meant training teachers in the use of the Museum's working textile machinery so that they may be able to undertake demonstrations without having to invoke the services of the Museum's education staff. To facilitate this, a range of information pamphlets has been produced, aimed specifically at the teachers, and intended to assist them in the practical process of acquiring a degree of basic skill. The other example is drawn from Sheffield schools museum service, where the structure of in-service teachers' courses is two-tiered in nature. At the first stage, simple courses are offered in how to plan a visit to the City Museum, and the branch museum at Abbeydale Industrial Hamlet also offers a one-day teachers' course, which includes a detailed tour of the site. A more ambitious second level course at Abbeydale is available for those teachers who have previously attended and who wish to make a study of the steel industry in greater depth.

Leisure activity

Museums are increasingly developing a side of their work which enables children to undertake various holiday and spare-time activities. For example, during school vacations the Victoria and Albert Museum organizes special projects of all kinds for children in three age groups that range from five to sixteen years. Other museums do likewise, and their efforts are often artistically or literary inspired. The Geffrye is an instance of this, with its extensive leisure activity services that make provision for painting, pottery, basketry and model making. Still, a great many of such services as are provided have a historical slant. Norwich and Oxford are two places which organize summer expeditions of archaeological interest, while the Geffrye, in pursuit of historically based studies, even makes its own arrangements to conduct small groups of local children on visits to other centres, such as the Science Museum in South Kensington or the Palace of Hampton Court.

Some museums make provision for children to be accommodated on Saturday mornings throughout the year. Typical of this is Bristol, which has a 'Junior Saturday Club' in which a varied programme offers opportunities for making replica armour as well as participating in ancient crafts like candle making. In Colchester, a particularly commendable degree of school—museum linkage has been achieved as a result of mutually fostered co-operation. Museum technology has provided the meeting ground, and pupils of some secondary schools in the area have become involved in pottery restoration and in the conservation of old machinery. For those in the upper age range of the school, this can be an exercise that is both educative and socially useful. As such, it is the kind of activity which could well be integrated into a broader-based historical or environmental study.

Some museums also encourage the co-operation of schools by organizing periodic competitions, simple or elaborate in nature. In some instances they are held during vacations, but the pattern which has found favour at Bristol is one in which submissions are required before the end of the session and in which two categories of entry are encouraged, individual and class. Five or six options may be offered from which either the class or the individual pupil may choose. In pursuing the topic of choice, pupils are expected to 'make an illustrated study which may include models'. This is the wording of one of the options:

> Much of Bristol is being altered and redeveloped; choose an area, a group of buildings or an individual building which you would like to see preserved, with your reasons for doing so, which may include comparisons.

Such an exercise, undertaken properly, invites the pupil to employ historical skills and, in sponsoring work of this kind, museums are doing much that is worth while in fostering a feeling for the past.

Handling

One issue on which there is likely to be divided opinion, and perhaps even confusion in the minds of teachers, is the desirability of allow-

museum education department

City Museums and Art Gallery Birmingham B3 3DH

EASTER HOLIDAY ACTIVITIES FOR SCHOOLCHILDREN 1974

HOLIDAY COMPETITION

"The Birmingham Fire Brigade" — A competition for 5's to 15's will be available for a small charge from the Catalogue Stall from Monday, 8th April to Friday, 26th April.

Date	Time	Age Group	Event	Location
8th April and 9th April	1000 – 1600 1000 – 1200	ages 9 – 13	Create a fire-fighting diorama using the displays in the new Museum of Birmingham History for ideas.	Schoolroom
9th April	1400	ages 5 – 9	"Fireman Figures" — make your own in various materials.	Schoolroom
10th April	1000	Parents and and children over 8	A guided tour of the Central Fire Station	Meeting inside main gate of Central Fire Station
	1400	ages 9 – 13	Fire-fighting session" — a chance to handle, draw and discuss objects connected with fire-fighting.	Schoolroom
11th April	1000 – 1600	ages 10 – 15	"Rag Dolls" — make your own Victorian rag doll. Please bring cloth scraps and one old thick sock or stocking.	Schoolroom
17th April and 18th April	1000 – 1600 1000 – 1200	ages 10 – 15	"Decorate your own Egyptian Tomb" — create your own life-size Egyptian tomb painting.	Meet at Schoolroom
18th April	1400	ages 9 – 13	"Victorian Surprise" — a mystery session in the galleries.	Meet at Schoolroom
19th April	1000	ages 9 – 13	"Victorian Surprise" — a similar session to that held on April 18th.	Meet at Schoolroom
	1400	ages 5 – 9	"Creative Drama" — using objects connected with fire-fighting with Mrs. Hilda Blandford-Harris, A.L.A.M.	Schoolroom
22nd April	1000	ages 5 – 9	"Discovering Stones" — looking at and drawing interesting stones, minerals and rocks.	Schoolroom
	1400	Parents, children and friends	"Springtime in the Midlands" — an illustrated talk.	Lecture Hall

No tickets are required for the "Springtime in the Midlands" talk. Please note that accommodation is limited, so you should arrive in good time.

Admission to the schoolroom events and the Fire Station tour is by free ticket obtainable in advance from the Museum Education Officer. A **very limited number** will be available immediately prior to the sessions. This does **not** apply to the Fire Station tour. We regret that we **cannot** accept telephone bookings. Applications should be made on the attached booking form. Because of the great demand, we can only allow up to **two** tickets for the schoolroom events per child. Please give three choices in order of preference. Applications will be dealt with in strict rotation. Please note that children attending **all day** sessions should bring a packed lunch.

Programme of holiday activities, Birmingham City Museums and Art Gallery

ing children to handle loan material. Some museums find a way around the problem by carrying a stock of replica items. Nevertheless, not everything is provided in this form, so that decisions have to be made about the extent to which children are to be permitted to go beyond visual examination. The fact that many schools museum services make no explicit statement of policy about this in their literature would seem to imply that the decision is regarded as resting with the school or even with the particular class teacher. Some take precautions against damage to precious material by supplying it in display cases. This does not necessarily mean that the museum has a policy of forbidding the handling of material by children. For example, the schools service department of the Manchester Museum clearly states that one of its objectives is 'to enrich the school curriculum in as many ways as possible, especially by enabling children to handle, and study in detail, the actual objects under discussion at school'. To this end, a clear indication is given in the lists of loan material as to which specimens may be handled in school. This includes oil lamps excavated in Israel, fragments of Roman pottery, Neolithic axe heads, etc. On the other hand, specimens which are subject to fading are delivered in wooden boxes with glass fronts, while others are displayed in perspex cases, in order to combine safety with the maximum visibility.

Generally speaking, most museums now take the view that, whenever possible, handling should be encouraged, especially in situations where children could benefit from doing so and no damage to the item is liable to occur: a prehistoric flint tool might come into this category, whereas a delicate model of a sailing ship or a flimsy item of eighteenth-century dress would not. Another important factor to be taken into consideration is the irreplaceable nature of certain items. This could be anything from a Roman tear glass to a faded and brittle letter signed by Garibaldi, folk hero of the Italian Risorgimento. One would be ill-advised to place either on open display; on the other hand, there is nothing to prevent children from being allowed to approach close to such objects.

Let it be recognized, of course, that there are many items which it would be inappropriate for anyone to handle for the mere sake of doing so. The Burrell collection, for example, has magnificent tapestries, but they are emphatically not the kind of objects which one would happily allow people to handle; to do so would merely be to invite rapid deterioration without any advantages whatsoever. This observation perhaps serves to stress the point that, in attempting to settle the question of whether or not a specific exhibit should be subject to handling the decision can often be made in terms of common sense, discretion and appropriateness. Further, it is worth bearing in mind that no matter what the item may be, if handling is generally permitted it is likely in time to become soiled or marked. The trouble then arises from the need to clean it, because cleaning processes are almost always destructive. A precaution which teachers can take is to ensure that pupils always have clean hands and do not place the items in situations where they could be contaminated by paint, ink or anything else likely to cause damage.

Much of this exhortation is plain common sense and, in the main, it is the experience of museum staffs that schools do take care of the materials temporarily entrusted to their care. Because of this, handling is a practice which most museum custodians endeavour to encourage and, as an example of this, the effect on museum-based courses of a positive attitude towards the idea of children being allowed to handle exhibits is nowhere better shown than in the services offered by the Merseyside County Museums. Well-thought-out study sessions, conducted under the direction of a member of the museums' staff or a teacher, are so designed that handling is a natural activity within a variety of contexts. For example, courses on the theme of 'Early Man' allow for the handling of hand axes, knives, scrapers, burins and tanged arrowheads. Others, on the rise and decline of the eighteenth century Liverpool pottery industry, are explored, in part, through the handling and recognition of a range of sherds as a means of identifying the different types of ware produced; they include examples of rough earthenware, tobacco pipes, delftware and so on.

Where models are shown, there are obvious possibilities for handling which would otherwise not be conceivable. Costume is a particularly good example of this, and earlier reference was made to the use of replica child-sized costume at Reading. To make use of the original clothes would be to invite certain and early disaster, for they could not survive the amount of wear to which they would be subjected. On the other hand, replica clothing has a dual merit. First, it is made up in cloth that, by its very newness, is less vulnerable to any kind of wear than older material would be. Secondly, it is relatively expendable, as the reproduction costume could be made up again. In any case, who is to say that wearing the copy affords any less of a true historical experience than putting on the original? After all, there was a time when the original itself was new, so that, although the boy or girl of today may be denied the undoubted thrill of putting on the actual garment of a former age, by means of the substitute it may be possible to recreate the feeling which the first wearer may have felt. In the light of such possibilities, it is hardly surprising to find that Reading is not the only museum to have thought of the value of allowing children access to reproduction costume. Colchester and Essex Museum, for example, includes as part of its service to schools the 'costume lecture'. A number of such presentations are given to children in the eight to twelve age group, and cover several historical periods, ranging from the Roman to the Victorian. There can be no doubt that those interesting presentations are much enlivened by the on-the-spot opportunities that are given to children to dress up in the appropriate costume. The imaginative and forward-looking Geffrye Museum is another place where children can have this type of experience; when its full-time teachers take lessons in the period rooms it is often possible to dress two members of the visiting class in reproduction costume.

In a number of instances, thinking on the issues of handling and dressing-up has advanced to the point where it is felt that something beyond the lecture with incidental handling is needed. In this respect, the Derby Museum has demonstrated how the involvement of children can be taken a stage further. The medium through which this is achieved is the reconstructed historical setting. What the museum does is to recreate, as accurately as possible, something like a room setting appropriate to a particular period and, in order to do this, use is made of material, both original and replica, held in the museum's collection. Children are then invited into active participation in such a way as to bring them to a kind of imaginative contact with the period represented by the chosen setting. For example, the museum will create a medieval kitchen and dining room. This is furnished with a trestle table on which are trenchers, knives, spoons, replica medieval pottery and horn beakers, set against the background of a fireplace and cauldron, a steelyard and a rush-strewn floor. The room is lit by rushlights in holders, as well as a cresset lamp. In this environment, children in costume assist in the preparation and subsequent consumption of a green stew, a typical medieval recipe, in which eggs and cheese are served up in a bright green colour as a result of parsley staining. They undertake the ritual of setting places at tables, and the whole thing is carried out to a background sound of medieval music.

This is an interesting and novel way of involving children in the direct handling of material. The constraints imposed by limitations of space make it difficult for the Derby Museum to do other than mount one setting at a time, but alternatives which have been tried include a Stone Age cave, a Roman barrack block and a Victorian parlour. It is an imaginative approach which opens up possibilities not only for physical handling of material, whether in original or in replica form, but also for dramatizing, even if this is only to feel something, however fleeting and however contrived, of what it was like to wear medieval dress and serve at a medieval table. In this activity there are no skills involved, for we are impinging on the affective element in the child's education. Nevertheless, the study of history is not all cognition and, in seeking for our pupils this imagining and vicarious experience, we may be doing a great deal to fill out an otherwise bare and perhaps dimly perceived view of the past.

Finally, as an extension to the theme of handling material, it is worth considering briefly some of the interesting work currently being undertaken by the schools museum service based at Wakefield. Reconstruction or restoration is an activity which almost all museums have to carry out in some form or another from time to time. Here, the major task attempted by this particular schools service, and one which has proved to be remarkably productive, is the full restoration of Clarke Hall, Wakefield. In practical terms, this has meant the restoring of a seventeenth-century yeoman farmer's house and grounds to their original condition, for the specific educational use of children and young people. Country houses of this type and period were to a great extent self-sufficient units, growing their own food and providing wool and linen that had been processed through all the stages of production in the workshops of the estate itself. Much of the restoration work has, therefore, taken the form of reconstructing kitchen and workshop equipment from contemporary source illustrations. In these reconstructed and re-equipped rooms parties of visiting schoolchildren may practice cooking, dairy work, spinning and weaving in the manner of three hundred years ago. This is only one of a number of similar ventures which this enterprising schools museum service has developed. Like the work in Derby, it goes beyond the admission of children to galleries or the extension of permission to handle things either in school or museum. Here, there is active participation, carried to such a stage of revitalizing as to blur and render indistinct any categorizing which might otherwise be made between Clarke Hall as a museum and Clarke Hall as a historical site.

As we face the future and the increasing possibility of the development of resource-based learning within our schools, there is all the more need for improving and opening out such opportunities for collaboration among the relevant agencies that disseminate information or provide materials for teachers to use. Already there are heartening signs that, in some places, local authority resources centres, teachers' advisory panels and schools museum services are working together in harmony. It is a development that deserves to be encouraged in every possible way.

7

Project Work and the London Museum

Teachers who habitually engage their classes in project work know well that there are those occasions when a particular study suddenly takes off with an astonishing momentum. Often this is the product of a number of favourable elements, such as the receptiveness and motivation of the children, the enthusiasm of the individual teacher or the attraction of the subject. A great deal of inspiration and direction often comes from outside the school, and nowhere was this better demonstrated than in the work of the former London Museum. In view of this, the purpose of this short concluding chapter is to look at some of the results achieved by its very successful and imaginative schools museum service.

In this respect, one of the most rewarding growth points was the succession of holiday lectures which were a feature of the London Museum's schools service for a number of years. In Easter 1974, the theme was 'Digging up the Past', and on two separate occasions a lecture was given by the Museum Field Officer on the archaeological investigation of the Thames valley. The talk was illustrated with slides, and objects discovered by digging were handed around. Such was the reputation previously built up by the Museum, that the lectures were well attended and received with great enthusiasm. Much of the interest, however, lay in the subsequent activities, because not only did a group follow up the lecture with a visit to a city site where a dig was in progress, but further expeditions were set afoot for the summer, and a number of the older children promptly signed up to assist in excavations planned for the following summer vacation.

Other themes which aroused interest were both varied and stimulating. 'Talking Machines' was a Christmas presentation, in which children saw a range of instruments from phonographs to quadra-phonic tape machines; they were also able to hear the voices of famous people from the past. 'Moving Picture Toys', one of the Easter lectures, introduced the early history of the motion picture by looking at a wide range of fascinating gadgetry. The imaginative approach of this particular talk was even demonstrated in the style of the entry ticket. This took the form of a simple thaumatrope, which the child could take away and make up. This is a circular disc on either side of which are drawn two associated images; rapid rotation of the disc by means of attached threads allows both to be presented to the eye simultaneously. In this instance, the two subjects were a bird and a cage.

Left: London Museum holiday lecture
Right: London Museum Lecture admission ticket in form of thaumatrope

On an entirely different theme was the talk on 'The Street Cries of London', a presentation which invited audience participation in a number of ways that included not only listening and looking but also joining in singing rounds and eating the hot spice gingerbread

Hot Spice Gingerbread!
Mrs. Spencer's Gingerbread
(An original recipe)

½lb flour
3oz treacle
4oz butter or lard or a mixture of both
4oz sugar
teasp. bicarbonate of soda
teasp. ginger

Mode:

Let the ginger be freshly ground; put it into a basin with the flour, sugar and soda; and mix these ingredients well together; warm the butter and treacle together; then with a spoon work it into the flour, until the whole forms a nice smooth paste. Knead; roll it out to about ½ inch thickness and bake in a moderate oven for 15 minutes. Cut it into rounds about 2½ inches diameter.

A great authority in culinary matters suggests the addition of a little cayenne pepper in gingerbread; whether it be advisable to use this ingredient or not we leave our readers to decide.

Gingerbread recipe issued as part of London Museum schools project

specially prepared for the occasion and sold in the newly opened 'street' of Georgian shops.

An interesting set of notes on the London street cries was also made available, with comment on writers, composers and illustrators who made references to the cries in their works. One of a set of ten full-page illustrations that were also prepared, each based upon the seventeenth-century engravings of Marcellus Laroon, is reproduced here. It will be apparent that the possibilities for follow-up work in the classroom were obviously not only literary, artistic and musical, but culinary as well. Several London schools were able to use this excellent beginning as a 'firing stage' for further investigation into more of the colourful customs that belong in London's past.

"Ripe strawberries! a groat a pottle today"
The pottle, a tall basket, held four pints, and a groat was a silver fourpenny piece. The strawberries came from the market gardens around London.
This illustration is based on a late 17th century engraving by Marcellus Laroon.

London Museum, illustration for project on 'Street Cries'

Of all the themes promoted by the Museum in recent years, one of the most successful was the coal-hole cover study of summer term 1971. Unlike the other examples which have been briefly considered, this particular venture did not begin with a talk although, as we shall see, there was one at a later stage.

Coal-hole covers or, as they are known in the foundry business, coal plates[1] are the circular-shaped lids of cast iron which cover those holes in the pavement through which, in Victorian and Edwardian times, supplies of coal were tipped to the cellars below. Many are most elaborate examples of Victorian design and bear also information about foundries or ironmongers of the time. Conscious of the way in which those historically valuable items of street furniture were fast disappearing, the schools

Coal-hole cover from Exhibition Road, South Kensington

museum service under the direction of Mrs Mary Speaight initiated a survey of as many as possible of the remaining examples of those in the London area. The co-operation of schools was sought, especially of those in the Victorian parts of London, and they were invited to participate by sending in details of coal-plates in their own areas.

The method decided upon as offering the best form of permanent record was the rubbing. The undoubted attraction which a pastime like brass-rubbing can have for children was another reason for the choice of procedure. The logical step was, therefore, not only to ask schools to join in, but also to offer reasonably full instructions to them on how to go about the process of taking a coal-hole cover rubbing. This is a short extract from a three-page pamphlet which was prepared by the Museum for that purpose:

Materials to be used for this survey
Green wall paper 18 in. x 11 yds. 28p
White 50 gsm paper 30 in. x 10 yds. 30p   or
Cake of heel-ball, black or brick red. 45p

---

[1] Sometimes also called 'opercula', from the description applied to them in the late nineteenth century by Dr Shephard Taylor, an enthusiastic student of the subject.

These materials can be obtained from Phillips and Page, 50 Kensington Church Street, London W.6, 01-937 5839, or by prior arrangement (at least 3 days) from The London Museum. The paper for the rubbing should measure 18 x 20 in. (if green wall paper is used) and 15 x 20 in. (if white paper is used, i.e. half the width).

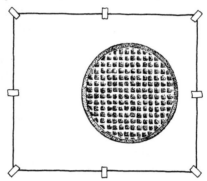

Diagram for placing the paper over the coal-hole

In addition to the rubbings themselves, details of provenance and frequency were also sought by the Museum, together with what was called, 'any other interesting discoveries'. The result was that thirty schools finally sent in rubbings, accompanied by information of the kind requested, such as the date when the street was laid out, the number of coal-holes which it had compared to the number of houses, or the names of the ironmongers' shops which were still in business and whose names were found on the coal-plates. An example of one such report is shown opposite.

Some children were also so sufficiently enterprising as to see applications beyond the simple requirements of the rubbing exercise. Mario Omar, aged ten, of the Princess May Primary School, investigated the possibilities of using printing ink and described the results as follows:

> ... we squeezed the oil printing ink on the coal cover and got the roller and rolled it all over the cover it only went on the raised part of the design then we got the T-shirt or apron or Skirt then we put the T-shirt on the coal cover then we got the clean roller and started to roll the Shirt and the design got on the Shirt then we took it off and made it dry 2 or 3 days.

> Gayton Road
>
> Gayton road was established in 1869.
> There are 53 coal holes in the street compared
> to 71 houses.
> There are 11 different coal-hole designs.
> John C. Aston Islington 70 Essex Road,
> R.H.J. Pearson Notting Hill and P.FEIL Stedall
> & son are some of the names of the makers.
> There were lots of coal-holes which were worn
> down by people walking on them.
> There were several coal-holes of the same
> design or a variation of the same design, close
> together.
> The houses were typically Victorian
> with wrought iron structures round
> the windows.

Part of the interest of the study stemmed from the fact that school pupils over a fairly wide age range participated. Nor were the basic courtesies overlooked, as is revealed in the illustration overleaf from a young child's work book: the children had been instructed by their teacher to observe at all times the niceties of polite behaviour by never intruding on private property without first asking the householder. Only one child from a group was to seek permission by knocking at the door; the others were to wait at the gate so as not to be a nuisance. It was reported that, while some ladies refused permission, most were happy to grant it and, in some cases, lemonade was given to the researchers. In the drawing, the householder is seen at the door, and the child sent as emissary has come back down the path to stand by the coal-plate; another pupil waits at the gate, and the teacher is depicted at bottom left.

Young child's illustration of coal-hole study activity

The project culminated in an eight-week exhibition at the London Museum, during which time many of the children's rubbings went on public display. Of the eighty-five schools which had expressed an initial interest in participating, something like 40 per cent submitted results, and at least one example from each was included in the exhibition. Visitors were also able to derive the fullest benefit from it by reading the set of notes which was made available to them and which had been built up around much of the information discovered by the children in the course of their investigations and recordings. This is an extract from them:

> The four rubbings from the Jones foundry at 80 Goswell Street (later known as 156 Goswell Road) illustrate the story of a foundry with a longer life. In 1850 James John Jones set up production at 80 Goswell Street. The second rubbing shows a plate made after he joined forces with Blaxton, a partnership lasting till 1863. The third plate must have been made between 1868 and 1885; in this year the business was expanded and named the Cannon Iron Foundry. It remained in existence until 1920.

Put together, the four rubbings in this example tell much, not only about the folk art of the period but also about the foundry with which they were associated.

It was, perhaps, appropriate that in 1972 the Easter lecture immediately following the completion of the project should have been on the theme of 'Rubbings' and have for its purpose the examination of possibilities extending beyond church brasses and coal-plates. For the 1971 project, itself, however, the most important material consequence was that the archives of the London Museum were enriched by the addition of the coal-hole rubbings made and donated by the schools. These now form a permanent record of an interesting element in the industrial archaeology of Victorian London, and the folders containing them bear on their covers the names of the schools responsible for the recording. Apart from the intrinsic value derived from active participation in a genuine piece of historical research, the nature of the study was such that the children were able to express themselves in an artistic and creative way. Encouraged also to look specifically for what they had hitherto either ignored or, at best, taken for granted, the exercise did much to bring them towards a fuller awareness of the physical environment within which home and school, the two focal points of their lives, were situated.

Throughout the sixty-two years of its existence, the London Museum remained Greater London's own special folk museum. Its principal concern was to illustrate the story of the growth from Roman times of one of the greatest capital cities in the world. Eastwards, in the Royal Exchange stood its sister institution, the Guildhall Museum, of greater antiquity but much more local in character, in that it tended to concentrate only upon those items firmly associated with the history of the City of London and its people.

In December 1976, those two places, which between them had well over two hundred years of history as local museums, ceased to have a separate existence and were amalgamated into one complex. This new, modern Museum of London, as it is called, stands at the corner of London Wall and Aldersgate Street, in the shadow of St Paul's. The principal exhibition galleries occupy 14,000 square metres of space, and in them are displayed the best of both collections, brought together for the first time to show the full and continuous story of London's two thousand years of existence. The renowned Roman and medieval relics from the Guildhall thus find their new home alongside the unrivalled collection of royal dresses, coronation robes and children's toys and games from the London Museum. Within this exciting new centre, the chronological pattern of London's story unfolds to show, through the exhibits, maps, models and reconstruction, the ever-changing scene that has made London what it is today. It is fitting that, within this context, a schools museum service of such undoubted enterprise and quality should be able to look to a future in which the opportunities for continuing with its imaginative and valuable work are likely to be greater than ever before.

Examples of Study Guide and Work Directive Material

The following examples have been chosen as illustrative of some of the best types of work material available for the use of children on visits to museums or historical sites. Four examples are given, each included because, in its own way, it exemplifies certain of the issues raised in the preceding text. With one exception, all are extracts from more extended pieces of work. The places to which they refer are:

British Museum: Department of Egyptian Antiquities
Fishbourne Roman Palace
Hereford and Worcester County Museum, Hartlebury
Bothwell Castle

British Museum: Department of Egyptian Antiquities

Example of study guide material

The British Museum, which was established in 1753, is today regarded as one of the great world museums. Its massive collections are wide-ranging and survey cultural development throughout the world, and at all stages of human history. Included among its treasures are many famed items, such as the Rosetta Stone, the Elgin Marbles, the Sutton Hoo ship burial, and the fourteenth-century Royal Gold Cup. For children, an outstanding attraction is the range of exhibits of the Department of Egyptian Antiquities, a collection which, in consequence of the skill and dedication of generations of scholars and collectors, is second in importance only to the Cairo Museum.

For the benefit of schoolchildren visiting this particularly inviting part of the Museum, much thought has been given to ways in which those rare survivals of early Near Eastern civilization may be seen and enjoyed. What follows is a short extract from one of a number of study guides prepared by the Museum's Education Service. Here the emphasis is much less on work direction and more upon guiding children round with the minimum of fuss and in such a way as to direct their attention to what might otherwise have been over-looked. It is not so much cognition as the well-springs of emotive response that are being tapped, and the compilers have clearly kept in mind this primary need to encourage and nurture the spirit of wonder. It is true that there is the occasional invitation to written activity, for example to try out hieroglyphs, but for the most part the concern is with looking, savouring and enjoying.

Royal cartouches of
Amenophis II,
Eighteenth Dynasty

HIEROGLYPHS

Apart from A and I sounds, the Ancient Egyptians did not write vowels. They spelled their names and words using consonants.

A

I - if
written twice
= Y

You might like to write your name as closely as you can in Hieroglyphs on the front cover of your booklet.

---

7 In Bay 10 on the right hand wall is a fragment from a tomb near the pyramids. What are the boys, men and donkeys doing?

8 Two large heads from statues of King Amenophis III, one of Egypt's richest rulers. How would you describe his expression?

9 In Bay 3 you will find a statue of King Sesostris III. Is his face like the other kings you have seen?

EXAMPLES OF STUDY GUIDE AND WORK DIRECTIVE MATERIAL

A (spoken gutturally)

W

B

P

UPPER FLOOR

B: SECOND MUMMY ROOM

Turn left into this room from the Persian Landing.

Look at the two free-standing cases on the right.

1. Here you can see an Egyptian who died over five thousand years ago. His body was buried in the sand along with his storage jars for the Afterlife. The heat dried up the body and preserved it in the condition you can see – even his auburn hair is still there.

2. There are two burials in this case. One is a skeleton of someone buried in a basket and the other is the skeleton of a young woman in a wooden coffin.

Around the walls are coffins for mummified bodies. Many are beautifully decorated inside and out. Pick out the one you like and draw the designs on it.

F

M

N

143

Fishbourne Roman Palace

Example of varied work directive material

A succession of excavations at Fishbourne has shown that the site was occupied in Roman times by a large building, dating from the end of the first century. The conclusions so far reached indicate that, until about the end of the third century, the Palace was in regular use, and was altered and added to during that time. Much of the site is owned by the Sussex Archaeological Trust, and part has been roofed over and opened to the public. Of the mosaic pavements which originally floored all the rooms, about a dozen remain, and some are very fine. In addition to this, half of the large, central garden has been laid out to the original Roman plan. In one corner of the public area a most instructive site museum has been established to show off the material discovered in the course of the excavations.

The *Young Students' Brief Guide* is a comprehensive booklet prepared by the Museum. It opens with pages of information, which include a ground plan and a chronology. Most of those which follow are work directive in nature, although a few are still concerned solely with presentation of factual material; some very attractive pages are also included for later work, either at home or back at school. The whole thing is arranged so that the child progresses systematically around the site, seeing in turn the three major areas of Museum, North Wing and Garden. Indeed, there is nothing to prevent a teacher from dividing the party into three groups, and starting each at a different point, with instructions to follow through in the order in which the items appear in the study direc-
tive. Illustration is well
used throughout, and
there is a glossary and a
checklist. The extract
shown opposite is one of
the pages from this very
attractive booklet.[1]

Sea-horse mosaic of the second century

[1]These extracts are taken from a guide now out of print.

DECORATED OIL LAMP

Wooden writing tablet filled with wax and stylus

Everyday things of the Palace

Samian pottery imported from Gaul

7ft.

18½ ft.

HOW TO WEAR A TOGA

About 6 feet of the 18½ feet edge is placed over the left shoulder, the curved side being outside. The remaining part of the Toga is passed round the body, under the right arm, and then thrown over the left shoulder as Fig. 2. The part which hangs down in front from the left shoulder is then pulled up under the fold across the body as Fig. 3.

Under the Toga was worn the Tunica, sometimes sleeveless, and used as an indoor garment for men and women.

Coin of Claudius reign often copied in Britain

ENGRAVED GEMSTONE

9

Hereford and Worcester County Museum, Hartlebury

Example of graded work directive material

Erected in 1675, Hartlebury Castle stands on the site of a former moated medieval castle. It underwent extensive restoration in 1964. Among the state rooms are a great hall with a portrait gallery and an eighteenth-century saloon in rócoco style. The north wing is used to house the Hereford and Worcester County Museum. The Museum collection is a small but comprehensive one, covering a fair range of material, related to the social and domestic life of the last three hundred years. Local geological, archaeological and industrial items are also represented. In the grounds there is a forge, a wheelwright's shop and a cider mill, together with a most interesting collection of horse-drawn vehicles which includes six gypsy caravans.

The Museum Education Service is forward-looking, with work directives which are among the best of their kind. These are divided into eight sets, and give full coverage of the Museum, including the outdoor exhibits. Of particular interest is the way in which questions have been graded at three levels of difficulty within each of the sets, representing, in part, a tendency to move from the concrete to the abstract and from greater to less reliance on straightforward factual questions. Nevertheless, this is purely a matter of emphasis because, as may be seen in the following example, even in the simplest directive (*a*), encouragement is given to comment and enquiry, while the one which is considered as the most exacting (*c*), still provides opportunity for factual recording alongside more penetrating observation. Another laudable feature of the Hartlebury directives is the inclusion, in each case, of suggestions for further associated activity.

Lead fountain mask by Bromsgrove Guild

HEREFORD AND WORCESTER COUNTY MUSEUM
Museum Education Service

QUESTIONNAIRE 6 (a)

CRAFTS AND INDUSTRIES

Here are some questions about the things you are going to see in
the Crafts and Industries displays. Answer them in your mind, and
write down your answers if your teacher asks you to.

Room 5

1. What do farmers use today, instead of scythes?

2. Can you see why one of the tools used to make needles
   is called a Duck Foot Knife?

3. Look carefully at the tools which cover one wall of
   the big gallery. What do you think most of them are
   made of?

4. Which is your favourite piece in the Bromsgrove Guild
   display? Why?

5. Now, go round to the loom-room (through the Kitchen and
   Measurement Gallery) and look carefully at the looms and
   the grain hoist. (This is above your head). Can you see
   any differences between the two looms?

6. What machine or machines do the work of a grain-hoist
   today?

FOLLOW-UP ACTIVITIES

(a)   Find out all you can about how needles are made.

(b)   Make a model of one of the looms or of the grain-hoist

HEREFORD & WORCESTER COUNTY MUSEUM
Museum Education Service

QUESTIONNAIRE 6 (b)

CRAFTS AND INDUSTRIES

Most of the items you can see here are still made in Worcestershire, although in some cases, the manner of their production has greatly changed during the past hundred years or so. The Bromsgrove Guild no longer exists, having closed in 1966, but its products can be seen all over the world.

There is a map of the County here, to show you where the various Worcestershire industries are in relation to each other. You will find the room illustrating the carpet industry and the grain-hoist, through the Kitchen and the Measurement Gallery.

1. Name three crops which used to be cut with a scythe.

2. Why is one of the needlemaker's tools called a Duck Foot Knife?

3. Why does a Smith need a forge?

4. What do you think was used as power to work the older loom in the Loom Gallery?

5. Can you see any differences between the two looms? If so, what are they?

6. (Look up). What machine or machines do the work of a grain-hoist today?

FOLLOW-UP ACTIVITIES

(a)   Find out as much as you can about the needle-making industry at Redditch, or, the carpet industry at Kidderminster.

(b)   Write a short account of a village blacksmith's work, and explain why he was such an important craftsman.

(c)   Draw, or make a model of one of the objects in the Bromsgrove Guild display, or, of one of the looms, or, of a grain-hoist.

EXAMPLES OF STUDY GUIDE AND WORK DIRECTIVE MATERIAL

HEREFORD & WORCESTER COUNTY MUSEUM
Museum Education Service

CRAFTS & INDUSTRIES

Questionnaire 6 (c)

Most of the items here are still made locally, though, of course, modern technology has revolutionised their manufacture. The Bromsgrove Guild no longer exists, having closed in 1966, but its products can still be seen all over the world.

(You will find the grain hoist in the room illustrating carpet industry, through the Kitchen & Measurement Gallery).

1. Why was it essential that the blades of scythes be made of steel, as opposed to iron?

2. Name 4 metals used to make the tools on the display-boards.

3. Sketch one of the objects made by the Bromsgrove Guild, or one of the spinning-wheels (the latter are in the Loom-Room).

4. Mention 3 major differences between the looms.

5. Why are grain-hoists no longer necessary?

FURTHER ACTIVITIES

1. Examine one of the following: (either in its present state, or trace its development from the beginning until now):

   (a) The carpet-making industry of Kidderminster;

   (b) The needle-making industry of Redditch.

2. Write a brief history (illustrated, if you like) of

   (a) wood spinning from prehistoric times until the Industrial Revolution;

   OR

   (b) saltmining in this area until c.1900

149

Bothwell Castle

Example of work directive material for an outside site

The castle, now in ruins, is one of the most impressive medieval remains in Scotland. The oldest surviving sections are from the thirteenth century, but there are particular dating problems due to the fact that two successive destructions took place during the Wars of Independence in the fourteenth century, on each occasion carried out by the Scots themselves! The main part is a large rectangular courtyard, enclosed by curtain walls, with flanking towers to south and east. Inside, on the east, are the remains of a hall and a chapel, but the west side is the point of greatest interest, where stands the surviving elements of a great circular donjon, isolated from the main courtyard by its own moat. The castle changed hands many times in the power struggles of the succeeding centuries.

The work directive which follows, effectively exploits the castle's great potential for field study work. Traces of initial incompletion, destruction, rebuilding and strengthening are all clearly discernible today, and a major strength of the directive is the way in which those features are made comprehensible to children. Another commendable aspect is the way in which pupil investigation is skilfully directed, for checking points are included in order to keep the young visitor on the correct route. With a site that is spread out, as this is, it is only too easy to go wrong, simply for want of a little guidance of the kind supplied here. It might also be noted that this is the first of a pair of directives on the castle. Here, the concern is only with the early building (thirteenth to fourteenth centuries). The second sheet, which is not shown, directs attention to the fifteenth-century parts. This too illustrates the skill of the compiler who, by being selective, has sought to avoid creating confusion in the minds of the children.

Arms of the De Moravia family, founders of the Castle

BOTHWELL CASTLE LANARKSHIRE

(Use this worksheet to guide you, putting a tick in each small square when you have seen the feature mentioned. Answer the questions in the spaces provided.)

Dates

1270   (roughly) Castle built for Walter de Moravia (Moray).

1297   Bothwell occupied by the English.

1298-9 Scots recaptured castle.

1301   Edward I recaptured castle, with help from Glasgow. Siege tower carried in pieces from Glasgow, assembled on the site and used successfully within two days (details from guide-book).

1314   (After Bannockburn) Scots re-took castle without a fight and partly demolished it.

1336   Edward III captured the site, and engaged John de Kilburn to rebuild it.

1337   Sir Andrew de Moray, Warden of Scotland, recaptured castle after a short siege, using siege tower, and dismantled it again, removing half the great tower.

1362   'Black Archibald', Earl of Douglas, rebuilt castle, and founded Church of Bothwell, which still remains. The buildings on the left of the courtyard were built after this.

1503   Castle visited by James IV (Feasting in the big hall with
& 1504 the row of tall windows).

1584   James VI took castle from its owners and kept it as a royal castle.

THE CASTLE OF 1270 AS PLANNED

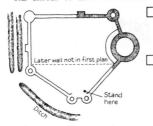

☐ These foundations are all that was ever built at this point. The huge round tower was completed and the wall and two towers on the far side of it (shaded).

☐ The ditch just behind you was dug out, and the approaches to the castle defended by wooden fences (PALISADES). These could be destroyed and rebuilt very quickly as happened in the Wars of Independence (1297-1337 above).

A LOOK AT THE OUTSIDE

From the gap in the big wall, where the wire fence is, turn right.
Follow the walls round until you can see the base of the great round
tower, or <u>DONJON</u>. ☐ (See ground plan below).

Notice how the walls have been demolished and rebuilt. The original
walls were made of smoothly cut, evenly shaped stones. The smoothest
stones are at the TOP/BOTTOM (Cross out the word which is wrong).
This means that the castle was repaired or finished CAREFULLY/IN A
HURRY. What was going on at the time which would cause this?
(See list of dates).

ANSWER_____

Look at the shape of the foot of the walls. What makes you think
that the walls were thicker at the bottom?

ANSWER_____

As you can see from the foundations, half the tower was pulled down
in 1337. The <u>STRAIGHT WALL</u> was put in as a repair shortly afterwards. ☐

Measure by tape measure or your own walking steps, the thickness of
the wall foundations.

ANSWER_____

Ground plan

☐ Original wall

☐ Foundations

☐ New wall

A LOOK AT THE INSIDE (Enter by gate in fence by custodian's hut)

1. Turn right towards the round donjon tower. The two windows facing into the courtyard with pointed arches are in the GOTHIC style. ☐

   DRAW a gothic window shape in the space provided.

2. Stand on the wooden footbridge and note :
   a) Below you on the right there is a POSTERN gate. ☐
   It was an escape route for defenders fighting on the drawbridge. Look carefully into the moat and work out how they would not be drowned if they escaped this way.

   ANSWER_____

   Say why you would still not like to escape this way._____

   b) The drawbridge fitted into a recess in the wall. Note the holes above the entrance for the cables ☐ which pulled it up.

   c) Right at the top of the tower over the doorway, there are the stone brackets for the HOARDING, ☐ a wooden platform which gave the defenders a chance to drop things on the enemy. It was daubed (French 'hourde') with clay to make it fireproof. There is room on the right for you to DRAW these stone brackets.

3. Enter the donjon, noticing the slots for the PORTCULLIS as you enter. ☐

   Note how the doorway faces along the wall and not into the open courtyard. ☐

   You cannot see from the drawbridge into the tower because the entrance passage ...... sharply to the right.

   (fill in missing word).

   All this helped the DEFENDERS/ATTACKERS.

4. Inside the donjon, <u>note the window</u> set in a recess in the wall, with wall ☐ seats on either side. Using the recess, you can measure the thickness of the wall which is _____ . This is THICKER/THINNER than at ground level. This window was part of the lord's hall, which had a wooden floor and a wooden ceiling. Higher up you can see <u>slots in the stonework</u> which were for the wood framework of the upper floors. ☐

At the far side of the hall, you can follow <u>a passage</u> in the thickness of the castle wall to the latrine tower. ☐

5. Returning to the hall, note the spiral staircase to the left of the main entrance. This leads down to the <u>basement</u>, which was a <u>store</u>, and contains the <u>well</u>. ☐

How would this help the defenders in a siege?

ANSWER _____

6. Using the spiral stair to the first floor level, go into the <u>chamber</u> over ☐ the portcullis and drawbridge. Note the <u>single arrow slit</u> (loop) which covers ☐ the approaches to the drawbridge. <u>Another</u> on the right commands the whole courtyard. ☐

Higher up, there is access to the wall top by a door which could be barred against anyone who forced his way into the donjon.
We can tell this because the doorway __

_____

(Try to explain how the door was shut)

Note the <u>beading</u> in the stonework over the doorway showing where the PENTHOUSE roof was – this was to protect those on the parapet from falling arrows. ☐

(See diagram)

Bibliography

Information on museums and historical sites

GOVERNMENT PUBLICATIONS (HMSO)

Sectional List No. 27: Ancient Monuments and Historic Buildings, revised 1 April 1976

List of Ancient Monuments in England and Wales, 6th edition 1973

* *List and Maps of Historic Monuments open to the Public*, 1972

Illustrated Regional Guides to Ancient Monuments in the Care of the State:

Vol. 1 *Northern England*, 2nd edition 1975

Vol. 2 *Southern England*, 2nd edition 1973

Vol. 3 *East Anglia and the Midlands* 2nd impression 1971

Vol. 4 *Wales*, 2nd edition 1973

Vol. 5 *North Wales*, 9th impression 1972

Vol. 6 *Scotland*, 6th impression 1970

Guide to London Museums and Galleries, 1974

Abbeys: An introduction to the Religious Houses of England and Wales, 5th impression 1972

Castles: An introduction to the Castles of England and Wales, 2nd edition 1973

Scottish Abbeys: an introduction to the medieval abbeys and priories of Scotland, reprinted 1970

Scottish Castles: An introduction to the Castles of Scotland, reprinted 1969

HM ORDNANCE SURVEY: archaeological and historical maps

General maps (dealing with specific periods or cultures)

Southern Britain in the Iron Age

Roman Britain
Britain in the Dark Ages
Britain before the Norman Conquest
Thematic maps (showing the distribution and character of certain features)
Ancient Britain
Monastic Britain
Individual monuments
Hadrian's Wall
The Antonine Wall

OTHER PUBLICATIONS
* *The Guide to Stately Homes, Castles and Gardens*, Automobile Association 1976
  The British Museum: a guide to its public services, Trustees of the British Museum 1970
  The World Museums Guide, COOPER, B. and MATHESON, M. Threshold Books 1973
* *Historic Houses, Castles and Gardens*, ABC Historic Publications, annual
* *London Guide*, Automobile Association 1971
  A Handbook to Roman London, MERRIFIELD, R. Guildhall Museum 1973
* *Museums and Galleries in Great Britain and Ireland*, ABC Historic Publications, annual
  The National Trust Atlas, National Trust 1964
  Properties of the National Trust, National Trust 1974
  The Family Guide on Where to Go, TITCHMARSH, P. and TITCHMARSH, H., Jarrold n.d.
  Treasures of Britain, Drive Publications 1976

  * inexpensive and particularly useful

Museums and historical sites related to the teaching of history

BOOKS
Museums and How to Use Them, ALEXANDER, E. Batsford 1974
Exploring London, BARNETT, I. Shell Junior Guide 1965

Museum School Services, CHEETHAM, F. W., ed. Museums Assoc. 1967

Patch History and Creativity, FAIRLEY, J. A. Longman 1970

Changing Museums, HARRISON, M. Longman 1967

Learning out of School, HARRISON, M. Ward Lock Educational 1970

Discovering Local History, IREDALE, D. Shire Publications 1973

Practical History Teaching, JAMIESON, A. Evans Brothers 1971

Meet Me in Trafalgar Square, KIRBY, M. Schoolmaster 1968

Museums in Education: Education Survey 12 Department of Education and Science HMSO 1971

Going to Museums, PALMER, J. Phoenix 1954

Discovering London for Children, PEARSON, M. M. Shire Publications 1971

Visiting Museums, WHITE, A. Faber 1968

Children and Museums, WINSTANLEY, B. Blackwell 1967

The Young Visitor's Guide to the Tower of London HMSO 1974

ARTICLES

'The museum and the school', *Teaching of History Leaflet No. 6*, BRYANT, M., Historical Association 1961

'The use of museums and historical sites' in *Handbook for History Teachers*, MAINSTONE, M. and BRYANT, M., ed., W. H. Burston, and C. W. Green, Methuen 1972

Useful addresses

Group for Educational Services in Museums, 87 Charlotte Street, London W.1 (for details of schools museum services in general)

Department of the Environment
 25 Savile Row, London W1X 2BT
 Receiver of Fees, HM Tower of London, London EC3 (Tower of London only)
 Depot Superintendent, DOE Hampton Court Palace, East Molesey, Surrey (Hampton Court Palace only)
 Five Ways House, Islington Row, Birmingham 15 1SL
 Radnor Road, Ancient Monuments Department, Bristol 7
 Ancient Monuments Administration, Government Buildings—Block 1 Gabalfa, Cardiff CF4 4YF

Lawnswood, Leeds 16 LS16 5PX

Seymour Grove, Old Trafford, Manchester 16 0JL

Government Buildings, Building B, Coley Park, Reading, Berks RG1 6DZ

Ashdown House, Sedlescombe Road North, Hastings, Sussex TN34 1XA

Block D. Brooklands Avenue, Cambridge CB2 2DZ

Sec S3 Room J707, Argyle House, 3 Lady Lawson Street, Edinburgh EH3 9SD

HM Ordnance Survey

Main agents

Cook Hammond and Kell Ltd., 22—24 Caxton Street, London SW1 HO QU (for England and Wales)

Thomas Nelson and Sons Ltd., 18 Dalkeith Road, Edinburgh EH16 5BS (for Scotland)

Other agents are situated in most large towns. List of those available on request from: The Director General Ordnance Survey, Department 32, Romsey Road, Maybush, Southampton SO9 4DH

National Trust

The National Trust, 42 Queen Anne's Gate, London SW1H 9AS

The National Trust for Scotland, 5 Charlotte Square, Edinburgh EH2 4DU

Government bookshops

49 High Holborn, London WC1V 6HB

13a Castle Street, Edinburgh EH2 3AR

41 The Hayes, Cardiff CF1 1JW

Brazennose Street, Manchester M60 8AS

Southey House, Wine Street, Bristol BS1 3BQ

258 Broad Street, Birmingham B1 2HE

80 Chichester Street, Belfast BT1 4JY

Select list of museums in London

Tower of London, Tower Hill, London EC3

British Museum, Great Russell Street, London, WC1B 3DG

British Museum (Natural History), Cromwell Road, South Kensington, London SW7 5BD

Victoria and Albert Museum, Cromwell Road, South Kensington, London SW7 2RL

Science Museum, Exhibition Road, South Kensington, London SW7 2DD

National Army Museum, Royal Hospital Road, London SW3 4HT

National Maritime Museum, Romney Road, Greenwich, London SE10 9NF

Imperial War Museum, Lambeth Road, London SE1 6HZ

Museum of London, London Wall, London EC2Y 5HN

Geffrye Museum, Kingsland Road, London E2 8EA

HMS *Belfast*, Symon's Wharf, Vine Lane, London, SE1 2JH

Select list of provincial museums

American Museum in Britain, Claverton Manor, Bath, Avon.

Bristol City Museum and Art Gallery, Queens Road, Bristol 8

Birmingham City Museum and Art Gallery, Congreve Street, Birmingham, B3 3DH

Leicestershire Museums, Art Galleries and Records Service, New Walk, Leicester

Merseyside County Museums, William Brown Street, Liverpool 3

North Western Museum of Science and Industry, 97 Grosvenor Street, Manchester M1 7HF

Castle Museum, York

National Railway Museum, Leeman Road, York YO2 4XJ

North of England Open-Air Museum, Beamish Hall, Stanley, Co. Durham

National Museum of Wales, Cardiff CF1 3NP

Welsh Folk Museum, St Fagans Castle, Cardiff CF5 6XB

Royal Scottish Museum, Chambers Street, Edinburgh EH1 1JF

National Museum of Antiquities of Scotland, Queen Street, Edinburgh 2

Glasgow Museum and Art Gallery, Kelvingrove, Glasgow G3 8AG

Ulster Folk and Transport Museum, Cultra Manor, Holywood, Belfast BT18 0EU

Index